Gerald Bray shares with h [...] riable ability to communicate pr [...] group of people. His treatment c [...] ching of Genesis, Matthew, John, [...] le and shows us how Chrysostom understood the outworking of the principle of accommodation in the Creator's communication with his creation. This introduction to Chrysostom will whet the appetite of those who want to see how one of the greatest preachers in the Christian church served the people God had given him to love.

—**Mark D. Thompson**, Moore College

John Chrysostom is a name too little known by Christians today, especially by Protestants. But this pastor from the late fourth and early fifth century is worth getting acquainted with and learning from. Thankfully, Gerald Bray has written an accessible volume that doesn't overwhelm us but instead helps us see how John interprets Scripture and applies it to life. Over his life John produced about six hundred sermons that we still have, but Bray wisely concentrates on four sections of Scripture (early Genesis, Matthew, John, and Romans) to give contemporary readers a real taste of wisdom from this ancient source. We may not agree with every move Chrysostom makes, but he certainly has a great deal to teach us.

—**Kelly M. Kapic**, Covenant College

John Chrysostom is one of those ancient Christian writers we think we know perhaps better than we do. Gerald Bray serves as a trustworthy guide to the essential Chrysostom, pointing the reader to key elements of the reluctant bishop's background as well as exploring the texts that will best introduce twenty-first-century readers to the "golden-mouthed" interpreter of Jesus, Matthew, John the Evangelist, and Paul.

—**Joel Elowsky**, Concordia Seminary, St. Louis

Today, so few Christians know the church fathers, let alone have read their writings. So I am ecstatic to see Gerald Bray retrieve a father like John Chrysostom, that golden-mouth preacher. Chrysostom not only defended the deity of Christ against Arianism but he also modeled sound biblical interpretation. Leaving us over six hundred sermons, pastors today will benefit from examining Chrysostom's rhetorical approach—especially in our day, when rhetoric has been exchanged for visual stimuli. But pastors and scholars alike also will be humbled by Chrysostom's refusal to preach the scriptures in a clever, sophisticated style, as if Christianity is only for elites. Chrysostom exemplified his Savior as well as the apostle Paul by preaching the scriptures with clarity. In doing so, Chrysostom imitated our incomprehensible Creator, who accommodated himself, even to the point of incarnation, to make his grace known. Read Bray on Chrysostom, and then go read Chrysostom for yourself!

—**Matthew Barrett**, Midwestern Baptist Theological Seminary

PREACHING THE WORD

WITH

JOHN CHRYSOSTOM

PREACHING THE WORD

WITH

JOHN CHRYSOSTOM

GERALD BRAY

LEXHAM PRESS

Preaching the Word with John Chrysostom
Lived Theology

Lexham Press, 1313 Commercial St., Bellingham, WA 98225
LexhamPress.com

Print ISBN 9781683593669
Digital ISBN 9781683593676
Library of Congress Control Number 2019957123

Series Editor: Michael A. G. Haykin
Lexham Editorial: Todd Hains, Jeff Reimer, Danielle Thevenaz
Cover Design: Micah Ellis
Typesetting: Abigail Stocker

23 xii / US

Contents

Timeline of
John Chrysostom's Life

347
Birth in Antioch

· · ·

360s
Tutelage under
Libanios

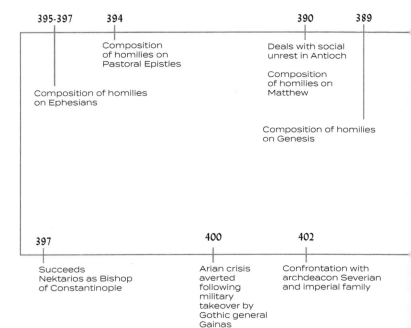

395-397
Composition of homilies
on Ephesians

394
Composition
of homilies on
Pastoral Epistles

390
Deals with social
unrest in Antioch

Composition
of homilies on
Matthew

389
Composition of homilies
on Genesis

397
Succeeds
Nektarios as Bishop
of Constantinople

400
Arian crisis
averted
following
military
takeover by
Gothic general
Gainas

402
Confrontation with
archdeacon Severian
and imperial family

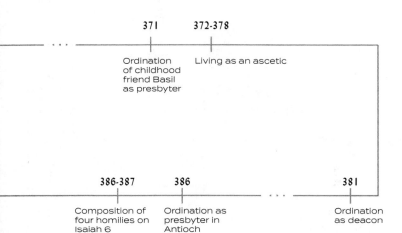

371
Ordination of childhood friend Basil as presbyter

372-378
Living as an ascetic

386-387
Composition of four homilies on Isaiah 6

386
Ordination as presbyter in Antioch

381
Ordination as deacon

403
Trial at The Oaks and first exile

404
Definitive exile with quiet departure from Constantinople

407
Death after forced march north into Armenia

LIVED
THEOLOGY

Series Preface

Men and women—not ideas—make history. Ideas have influence only if they grip the minds and energize the wills of flesh-and-blood individuals.

This is no less true in the history of Christianity than it is in other spheres of history. For example, the eventual success of Trinitarianism in the fourth century was not simply the triumph of an idea but of the biblical convictions and piety of believers like Hilary and Athanasius, Basil of Caesarea and Macarius-Symeon. Thirteen hundred years later, men and women like William Carey, William Ward, and Hannah Marshman were propelled onto the mission field of India—their grit and gumption founded on the conviction that the living, risen Lord has given his church an ongoing command: "Go therefore and make disciples of all nations, baptizing them in the name of the Father and of the Son and of the Holy Spirit, teaching them to observe all that I have commanded you. And behold, I am with you always, to the end of the age" (Matt 28:19-20). These verses had an impact when they found a lodging-place in their hearts.

The Lived Theology series traces the way that biblical concepts and ideas are lived out in the lives of Christians, some well known, some relatively unknown (though we hope that more people will know their stories). These books tell the stories of these men and women and also describe the way in which ideas become clothed in concrete decisions and actions.

The goal for all of the books is the same: to remember what lived theology looks like. And in remembering this, we hope that these Christians' responses to their historical contexts and cultures will be a source of wisdom for us today.

> *And these all, having obtained a good report through faith, received not the promise: God having provided some better thing for us, that they without us should not be made perfect. Wherefore seeing we also are compassed about with so great a cloud of witnesses, let us lay aside every weight, and the sin which doth so easily beset us, and let us run with patience the race that is set before us, Looking unto Jesus the author and finisher of our faith.* (Hebrews 11:39–12:2 KJV)

Michael A. G. Haykin
Chair and Professor of Church History
The Southern Baptist Theological Seminary

CHAPTER 1

John the Man

HIS LIFE

J ohn was born to a Christian family in Antioch, probably in or around the year AD 349.[1] His father died when he was still a boy, and he was brought up by his mother. He received an excellent classical education and was taught rhetoric by a man called Libanius, who was widely regarded as the greatest teacher of the subject at that time. When John was eighteen years old, he broke off his studies and tried to adopt a strict monastic way of life, much to his mother's distress. He was baptized about this time and eventually managed to escape to the nearby mountains, where he found refuge with a hermit. After four years in the hermit's cave, John branched out on his own. For two years he practiced the most extreme asceticism, doing considerable damage to his health in the process. In the end it was too much for him, and he returned to Antioch, where he sought medical help and went back to the church of his youth.

In 381 John was ordained a deacon by Bishop Meletius of Antioch, and five years later he was made a priest by Meletius's successor Flavian. For the next eleven years John preached regularly in the city's main church, and it was there that he acquired his enduring reputation as a preacher. His most famous sermons were delivered during those years, which in hindsight were the happiest ones of his life. He developed an expository style of preaching and seems to have worked his way through Genesis, Isaiah, and the Psalms in the Old Testament, along with Matthew, John, and the Pauline Epistles (including Hebrews) in the New.

John's reputation spread, and in 397 he was chosen to become patriarch of Constantinople, the capital of the Eastern Roman Empire. John did not want to go, but the emperor intervened and forced him to leave Antioch. On February 26, 398, he was consecrated a bishop in his new see, but it turned out to be an unfortunate choice. Constantinople was a hotbed of corruption and political intrigue, and John was too forthright to be able to negotiate its treacherous byways successfully. He condemned the moral laxity of the city without compromise and did what he could to reform the church, which had succumbed to its atmosphere. By deposing unworthy bishops and clergy he made enemies who became increasingly determined to get rid of him, and his denunciations of the imperial court's luxury and decadence earned him no friends there either. In particular, the empress Eudoxia turned against him, having been convinced by John's enemies that his criticisms were directed mainly at her.

John also faced problems caused by the rivalry between Antioch and Alexandria. He had been consecrated as patriarch by Theophilus of Alexandria, but the latter was acting under duress, having been forced by the emperor to perform the ceremony. A few years later, Theophilus was summoned to Constantinople to answer charged leveled against him by some Egyptian monks. The trial was presided over by John, and Theophilus came to believe that the whole affair had been instigated by him. Seeking revenge, Theophilus summoned a meeting of thirty-six bishops, twenty-nine of whom were Egyptians like himself, in order to try John on a series of trumped-up charges. The strategy worked, and in August 403 he was deposed, a decision that the emperor lamely accepted.

John was expelled from the capital, but he was recalled the very next day when riots broke out in the city in his defense. John was restored to his office, and things seemed to be patched up, but two months later he was again accused of attacking the empress. This time the accusation stuck. The emperor ordered John to retire from his functions, but John refused to do so, and trouble soon followed. John had many followers in Constantinople, and when the army tried to expel him from his church the congregation resisted, with some loss of life. The situation became intolerable, and on June 9, 404, five days after Pentecost, John was forced to leave the city. He was exiled to the Armenian town of Cucusus (now Göksun in south central Turkey), where he lived for the next three years.

Unfortunately for John, Cucusus was not all that far from Antioch, and his former parishioners were soon making the pilgrimage to visit him, along with some dedicated followers from Constantinople. Nor was Cucusus a safe place for someone of John's stature to reside. It was subject to periodic raids by the mountain men of nearby Isauria, and John had to flee from them at least once during his stay there. The support that he received from both Antioch and Constantinople alarmed John's enemies, who had the emperor banish him to Pityus (now Pitsunda in the Abkhazian region of Georgia). Forced to go there on foot, and exposed to the hardships of bad weather and a semidesert terrain, John never made it to his destination. On September 14, 407, he died in Comana Pontica, a city that lay near modern Tokat, about halfway between Cucusus and the Black Sea, and is now in ruins.

John's death came to be seen as a form of martyrdom, and his fame spread. A century after his death he became known as Chrysostomos ("golden mouthed") because of his gift for preaching, and the name has stuck. The Roman church broke off relations with Constantinople because of what happened to John, and it was not until the wrong done to him was put right that relations between the two largest churches of the Christian world were restored. Thirty years after he passed away, John's remains were brought back to Constantinople, and the emperor Theodosius II (408–450), the son of Arcadius and Eudoxia, publicly begged forgiveness for his parents' sin in opposing John's ministry. In later times John became the best loved of all the Greek fathers of the church, and his extensive legacy has been preserved almost intact. The simplicity of his life, the sincerity of his faith, and the sufferings he was unjustly forced to endure all combined to enhance his reputation, which was particularly strong among the Protestant Reformers of the sixteenth century, who regarded him as a model Christian leader.

John's reputation began to suffer in the late nineteenth century, when interest in the early church period turned more toward studying the history of Christian doctrine. John was not particularly involved in any of the great theological controversies of his time, though he was a convinced and consistent defender of Nicene orthodoxy. His pastoral approach left the impression that his theology was simplistic, and some scholars started to wonder whether he could be called a theologian at all. The result is that today John is little known and seldom read. There are few recent translations of his writings, and it is only quite recently that interest in them has started to pick up again, partly because of a renewed concern for patristic biblical interpretation. Whether this will lead to a renewed interest in John as a preacher remains to be seen, though it is probably true to say that this is unlikely to occur unless it is accompanied by a more general revival of interest in preaching.

HIS WORKS

John wrote a few treatises on moral and pastoral subjects, and he has left us a fair amount of correspondence, but his reputation rests mainly on the large number of his sermons that have survived. Unfortunately for us, his fame as an orator was such that many people sought to imitate him, and much of what later circulated under his name comes from these admirers rather than from him. The task of sorting out the genuine sermons from the spurious ones remains unfinished, and there is as yet no critical edition of his works, which puts him at a disadvantage when compared with great contemporaries like Athanasius and the Cappadocian fathers (Basil of Caesarea, Gregory of Nazianzus, and Gregory of Nyssa). There is also a difficulty regarding translations. By no means all of John's vast output is available in English, though his expository sermons on the New Testament were published between 1888 and 1893 in five volumes of the *Library of Nicene and Post-Nicene Fathers*. The translation style is somewhat archaic for modern readers and makes John seem old fashioned and occasionally obscure, but there is nothing comparable available elsewhere. John's sermons on the Old Testament and his other writings are only partially translated, and much remains to be done to make them accessible to modern readers.

Surprising though it may seem, John's reputation has also suffered from the fact that most of his sermons are expositions of Scripture. One reason for this is that his expository style seldom attracts the interest of modern biblical scholars, whose work is based on different hermeneutical principles and often leads to quite different interpretations of the texts. More significantly, John's applications of those texts, while it had a powerful effect in his day, is frequently hard for later generations to appreciate because of the very different circumstances in which we now live. Nevertheless John's methods and principles often remain valid, even if many of the details now seem obscure or irrelevant, and it is by examining them that we can rediscover his genius and its ongoing importance for preachers in every age.

A difficulty with reading sermons is that it is impossible to recapture the original atmosphere in which they were preached. John's use of gestures, his tone of voice, his sense of humor, his allusions to contemporary events that are unknown to us now—all of these are lost to the modern reader. Nor can we be sure to what extent the texts we have represent what he actually said. Some of them may have been reproduced verbatim in written form, but it is probable that most of them were edited, either by John himself or by a literary executor. It is also possible that some of the sermons were never actually preached but were prepared directly for publication, using a standard homiletical format. We must therefore be careful not to assume too much about his preaching style, which may have been somewhat different from what the surviving evidence suggests. At the same time, John's live presentation cannot have been so different from the texts as to make it unrecognizable. We can be fairly certain that his imprint is stamped over the surviving sermons to a degree that makes them authentically his, even if we cannot recapture his original delivery.

John's most important sermons are expository ones on different books of the Bible. He was not the only church leader who preached in that way, but he was a master of the genre whose sermons were preserved when those of most others were for-gotten. From the Old Testament we have seventy-six sermons on Genesis, subdivided into two collections. The first consists of eight homilies on Genesis 1–3 with a ninth that ranges over the remaining chapters. The second collection covers the entire book, with much of the material from the first series repeated almost word for word. We also have fifty-eight sermons on selected psalms and a complete series on Isaiah that survives only in an Armenian translation.[2] In addition to that, there are isolated sermons on Hannah, the mother of Samuel, on David and Saul, and on Elijah, along with extensive fragments of hom-ilies on Job, Proverbs, Jeremiah, and Daniel.

From the New Testament, John has left us the first complete commentary on Matthew, which he covered in ninety sermons, and eighty-eight on the Gospel of John. He also produced fifty-five sermons on the Acts of the Apostles, the only commentary on that book to have survived from ancient times, as well as a collection of 244 sermons on the Pauline Epistles, including Hebrews.[3] Most of these were delivered in Antioch, though the seventy-seven homilies on Philippians, Colossians, 1 and 2 Thes-salonians, and Hebrews date from his time in Constantinople, as does the series on Acts. There are also a number of stand-alone sermons on particular passages, many of them tied to events in the life of Jesus that are commemorated in the liturgical year.

In all, John has left us about six hundred sermons on spe-cific biblical texts, but we must note that these include about 18,000 references or clear allusions to other parts of Scripture as well. John never quoted Ruth or the short epistles of 2 and 3 John, and there are other books that he mentioned only once (Ezra, Esther) or twice (Nahum). But this seems to be acciden-tal and does not indicate that he rejected their canonicity. John also accepted the Old Testament Apocrypha as Scripture, but he seldom used it. There are only three sermons on 1 and 2 Maccabees, for example, and a few quotations from other apocryphal books elsewhere. Like most of the church fathers, it seems that John regarded the Apocrypha as inspired because it was part of the Greek Old Testament (Septuagint), but he had little use for it in practice and never preached on it systematically.

Looking beyond the sermons that were specifically expository, we find that John preached against both Arians and Jews, and that he often denounced contemporary immorality in diatribes devoted to such evils as the theater and the circus games. A number of sermons dedicated to preparing candidates for baptism have survived, as have occasional pieces composed to celebrate various liturgical feasts or to honor the memory of great saints and martyrs. Especially notable among these are seven sermons in praise of the apostle Paul, whom John admired and with whom he felt a particular kinship, perhaps because they were similar personalities.[4] Occasionally John stepped directly into the political arena, as when he preached a series of twenty-one sermons dealing with the destruction of the imperial statues by an Antiochene mob in 387. The emperor threatened to destroy the city in retaliation, but the intercession of Bishop Flavian persuaded him to show mercy. John's interventions were evenhanded. He deplored the emperor's thirst for vengeance and prayed that it might be stayed (as it was), but he also castigated the Antiochenes for their behavior, which had brought down condemnation on them. Later on, in Constantinople, he preached in favor of the disgraced imperial minister Eutropius, who had been his friend and mentor before his fall from power. John could not save the minister, but Eutropius was exiled to Cyprus rather than put to death, which in the circumstances may be considered a success.[5]

John also wrote several treatises on the priesthood, the monastic life, virginity, the education of children, and suffering, many of which became popular devotional works in later times. Significantly, the Greek Orthodox Church has a Liturgy of St. John Chrysostom, which it celebrates on particular feast days, but how much of it goes back to John himself is uncertain. Most of the other works that survive under his name, including an important (but unfinished) commentary on Matthew, are now regarded as spurious.[6]

READING CHRYSOSTOM TODAY

With such a vast array of material to choose from, deciding where to begin reading John is extremely difficult. In the past, many students have chosen to concentrate on particular treatises, especially the ones on priesthood, because they have felt that in them John was addressing subjects that were still of great interest and relevance to modern church life. But important as they are, those treatises do not represent the heart of John's labors. For him, expounding the Bible from the pulpit and applying its lessons to the lives of his congregations remained his fundamental concern throughout his life, and to understand him properly we must begin with them.

Even so, it is scarcely practical to try to cover everything. Limitations of space force us to be selective, and most scholars would probably agree that this is best done by concentrating on four key texts—the creation narrative in Genesis 1-3, the Gospels of Matthew and John, and Paul's Epistle to the Romans. The creation narrative was a favorite theme of patristic commentators and is important because it established the worldview of Christianity over against the received wisdom of the pagans. Today, when the church is once again facing challenges from a secular culture that rejects the biblical doctrine of creation, this emphasis needs to be recalled in the hope of learning lessons from the past that may help us to resolve the conflicts of the present.

The Gospels of Matthew and John are self-evidently important because they recount the life and teaching of Jesus, albeit from different perspectives. John Chrysostom's exposition of them reveals his doctrine of Christ, which is that of Nicene orthodoxy, and which remains central to the life of the church today. His exposition of Romans is widely regarded as his best work, and it gives us an insight into John's deep affinity with the apostle Paul. It also speaks to the perennial controversies inherent in the Christian faith—the nature of original sin, the relationship of Jews to gentiles in the divine plan of salvation, and justification by faith alone. These themes remain as vital to our understanding of the gospel now as they have ever been, and it would not be surprising if modern readers resonate with John more fully in the sermons where he is discussing them than elsewhere in his writings.

What I propose to do is to work my way through each of these four texts, outlining how John read them himself, how he expounded them to his hearers, and how he applied them to the Christian life. Once beginners have mastered these principles, they will be ready and able to tackle the rest of John's legacy, secure in the knowledge that they understand where he is coming from and able to interpret what he says in a way that is faithful to his intentions. We have to remember that John was a fallible human being who lived a long time ago, and we should not expect to be able to follow him uncritically, but in spite of everything there is enough in his works that transcends the limitations of time and space and allows us to experience the communion of saints that unites us all in the eternal body of Christ.

JOHN CHRYSOSTOM'S MINDSET

To understand where John was coming from in his preaching, we have to consider what his intellectual background was and what he was trying to communicate to his congregations in his sermons. All forms of literature are products of their time, and it is only if they can speak not only to the original hearers but also to the second and third generations that read them that they are likely to survive beyond the circumstances in which they were produced. If this is true of books, it is even more true of speeches, and sermons are a particularly focused form of speech. Preachers do not necessarily look beyond their immediate congregations, but even if they do, they know that they must first persuade the people sitting in front of them of both the truth and the importance of what they have to say. That John's sermons should have survived in the quantity that they have is an impressive testament to their worth, but even so, modern readers will inevitably find it difficult to enter fully into the spirit of his preaching. We are obliged to read what was originally a three-dimensional performance in a one-dimensional format, a handicap that we must try to overcome by looking carefully at the background John came from, and at the expectations that both he and his hearers would have shared.

Today we live in an audiovisual world in which the spoken word is reduced to a minimum. Tweets and sound bites have replaced lectures and speeches, and for most people, a twenty-minute sermon is the most extended form of address that they are likely to hear on a regular basis. To make things even more difficult for the modern preacher, congregations are not trained to listen to and absorb what they hear, so they are easily distracted or bored. Preachers nowadays usually have no training in rhetoric and have to learn from experience what communicates to their congregations and what does not. John Chrysostom lived in a different world. In his time, oratory was highly prized, people were generally attentive to what they heard, and speakers were taught how to use their voice to best effect. Not everyone succeeded to the same degree, of course, but expectations were great and standards were high. John inherited a long tradition of public speaking that went back to ancient Greece, and in particular to the great Athenian orator Demosthenes (mid-fourth century BC), who made his name by opposing the expansionist plans of King Philip II of Macedon, the father of Alexander the Great.

Demosthenes was not just an ideal from the distant past but a model that John and his contemporaries were expected to imitate. In this endeavor he was universally acknowledged to have been one of the most successful, managing to produce a form of words so pure in its classical style that it could have come from seven centuries before his time. The amazing thing is that John achieved this without sounding stilted or archaic to his contemporaries. Where others indulged in high-flown rhetoric, he kept everything simple and straightforward, recognizing that most people were put off by technical theological jargon that they could not understand. In modern times that approach has often been seen as lowbrow, but in reality he had mastered the essence of the classical style, which was to present complex ideas in a simple way that spoke to educated and uneducated alike.

John believed that this was essential, because the church included every class of society. One of the failings of classical Greek culture is that it was elitist. Schools of philosophy gathered around men like Plato and Aristotle, but while these disciples imbibed and developed their master's ideas, they paid little heed to the needs of ordinary people. To be a philosopher was to rise above the common herd and discourse of things that the less enlightened knew nothing of. To be fair, that was not the view of Plato himself. He believed that the purpose of education was to raise up teachers who could then reach down to the level of the uneducated and lift them up to a similar level of enlightenment. But the experience of centuries had clouded that idealistic vision. The philosophers of John's day spoke to nobody but themselves, and too many of his fellow Christians were tempted to follow suit.[7] John resisted this trend, with the result that he achieved fame not just as a theologian but also as a popular communicator who made Christianity comprehensible to a generation that (in many cases) was hearing it for the first time.

From the Christian point of view, classical Greek education was deficient in two fundamental respects. First of all, the philosophers did not know what they were expounding. They speculated about the nature of the universe and claimed to have acquired a higher understanding of it than ordinary mortals had managed to acquire, but they could only guess as to what ultimate reality might be. Some said it was spiritual; others, material. Some claimed that it was eternal; others thought that it was in constant flux as time took its toll. Nobody knew the truth, even though rival schools of thought did not hesitate to proclaim their views as definitive (and condemn those of their rivals). Christians, by contrast, knew what they believed, not because they had guessed right, but because the truth had been revealed to them in the writings of the Hebrew prophets and the testimony of the apostles of Jesus Christ. The Bible, as we now call this collection of texts, is a coherent explanation of reality, and for a man like John Chrysostom, the primary duty of the Christian preacher was to expound what it meant and to apply its teaching to the lives of believers.

In sharp contrast to the elitism of classical Greek culture, the Christian church was a fellowship that embraced all types and conditions of humanity—rich and poor, Greek and "barbarian," male and female, young and old—everyone. The pagan philosopher could address a chosen few, but the Christian preacher had to speak to the whole range of his hearers, bringing God's word to bear on intellectuals and nonintellectuals alike. It did not matter to John if a few highly educated snobs looked down on divine revelation as uncouth and simplistic. What he cared about was that it should be intelligible to all because it was intended for all, and as Scripture itself reminds us, it is often the poor and apparently foolish who shame the wise by their understanding of the deep things of God (1 Cor 1:26–31).

John's calling to reach the full range of humanity was fortified by yet another basic principle of Christian belief. The philosophers had striven to achieve an intellectual synthesis that, by definition, was liable to be understood only by those who were capable of stretching their minds to absorb it. But the Christian God was unfathomable by even the cleverest intellect. Between the realm of the divine and that of the human there was a great gulf fixed, the gulf between the Creator and his creatures that none of the latter was able to bridge. A Platonist might pride himself on being more intelligent than the average peasant, and perhaps he was, but when the two stood before the living God they would be reduced to the equality that comes from being a sinner in need of grace. Neither the philosopher nor the man in the street could begin to probe the depths of the divine wisdom. Christian belief was not the fruit of academic labor but of spiritual awakening, and that awakening could come to the humblest and most unlikely people. Speaking of the apostle John, Chrysostom says,

> This completely ignorant man, who never went to school either before or after becoming a disciple of Christ—let us see what he says and what he talks to us about. Is it about things in the fields? Or about things in rivers? Or about the fish trade? We might expect that sort of thing from a fisherman, but that is not what we get. Not at all! Instead, we hear about the things of heaven, things that nobody ever found out before he revealed them. ... Is this natural for a fisherman? Do orators speak this way? What about sophists and philosophers, or those who are trained in pagan wisdom? No. The human mind is simply incapable of philosophizing on the nature of heaven and what belongs to it.[8]

Spiritual awakening is the gift of God working through his Holy Spirit in the life of the church. As the apostle Paul explained to the Corinthians, there are different callings and ministries, but the same Spirit is present in all who believe. Like most people in the early church, John thought that the gift of the Spirit was given in baptism, but while modern readers might find this understanding too simplistic, Christians today will agree with him that it is only by the Spirit of God at work in our hearts that we can come to understand the gospel of Christ and take it into our lives.[9]

The fact that the church embraces all sorts of people means that its ministers must also serve them as fully and as impartially as possible. For John this meant giving special consideration to the poor, the socially outcast, and those who for one reason or another have been victimized by society. But it also meant castigating the wealthy and powerful, who were liable to abuse their standing and ignore the needs of those less fortunate than themselves. John believed that every household should reflect Christian values, with the weak being supported by the strong and with everyone learning the basic principles of Christian living by practicing them on a daily basis. The role of the pastor was to edify the church, both by his teaching and by his example. John's model for this was the apostle Paul, whom he saw as the supreme exponent of the Christian life. Indeed, it is perhaps not too much to say that John regarded Paul much in the way that Paul regarded Jesus, as an example to imitate as far as possible in every situation and relationship.

JOHN'S HERMENEUTICAL PRINCIPLES

John Chrysostom taught that the Bible was revealed by God by means of a process that he called "accommodation."[10] Accommodation is a teaching technique made necessary by the fundamental divide between the infinite Creator and the finite creation. Human minds cannot understand the divine in the pure or absolute sense, because our finite minds are not adapted to the infinite. Any human attempt to create an absolute being or value will end in idolatry, because the only way that this can be done is by turning something that is finite into something that is not. The resulting distortion is sin, and is characteristic of all non-Christian beliefs. But God has created human beings in his own image and likeness, making it possible for the gap between us to be bridged in some way—not by us, but by him. God reaches out to us by choosing words and pictures to represent something of himself in a way that we can understand. The obvious example is that he tells us that he is our Father, borrowing a human concept to explain something that is true of him. Of course, as John and all his contemporaries insisted, this is an analogy that must not be pressed too far—there is no divine Mother, and we do not share the same being with God in the way that we do with our human parents. Even so, there is a relationship between us that can be compared to the relationship that a human father has with his children. God cares for us, provides for us, and makes us coworkers with him in his kingdom, and so we are not wrong to think of him in the way that he reveals himself to us in the Bible.

One tricky area that John had to tackle was the fact that analogies can sometimes be lies. A human example (which he did not use) is the way in which parents often explain where babies come from to children who are too young to understand the unvarnished truth. Parents create stories to explain this, but obviously none of these stories would stand up to scientific analysis. Such "lies" are justified, John thought, because they serve a higher purpose. Babies obviously do come from somewhere, and when children are old enough to understand, they will be told the truth. At that point they will be expected to abandon the myths of their childhood and embrace the facts, a process that Paul alluded to in 1 Corinthians 13:11.

This, said John, is the way in which God has dealt with his people. In the Old Testament God had to speak to the Hebrews as children, telling stories and establishing ritual practices that were not ends in themselves but that pointed to a higher reality that was eventually revealed in Christ. Thus, for example, the people were commanded to sacrifice a lamb for their sins, even though the blood of an animal could never atone for the misdeeds of human beings. Even the apostle Paul used pictures to make his points, John claimed, because many of the people to whom he preached were incapable of understanding the straightforward reality of the gospel. An example that he gives is the way in which Paul became "a Jew to the Jews." Christianity was a replacement for Judaism, the grown-up version, if you like, of what had been revealed in a childlike way in the Old Testament. Paul was not really a "Jew," and he did not advocate keeping the law of Moses—rather the reverse—but in order to make contact with those for whom Moses was the primary spiritual authority, he was prepared to adopt Jewish ways so that he would be accepted by those to whom he wanted to preach.[11]

It was this consideration that led him to circumcise Timothy (Acts 16:3), even though he did not believe that circumcision was of any spiritual value and effectively abolished it in the life of the church. So far, the modern reader can follow John without difficulty. But John goes on to say that by circumcising Timothy, Paul was deliberately deceiving the Jews in order to gain their confidence. Once he had obtained that, he then set about demolishing the very thing that he had used to appeal to them. John actually called this "deception," and what is more, he commended it to Christians as a perfectly proper way to behave. As we would say today, "The end justifies the means." But does it? Here most modern readers would feel uncomfortable, even if they agree with John that Paul had Timothy circumcised for pragmatic reasons and that he had no desire to make circumcision compulsory for Christians. But at the same time, we would almost certainly deny that this accommodation to Jewish sensitivities was a form of deception because we would not accept that circumcision is wrong—merely unnecessary. Jewish Christians can keep aspects of the Mosaic law if they want to, but they are not obliged to do so and cannot force others to observe their particular customs.

To understand the significance of this, we need only look to the advice Paul gave to Christians who had to face "weaker brethren" (almost certainly Jews) who could not in good conscience eat meat that had been sacrificed to idols. Paul's approach was essentially pragmatic. There is no need for Christians to eat such meat, he said, and if it offends some people, it is better not to do it. Paul's advice in that situation was not intended to deceive anyone, and there is no suggestion that he was hoping to soften up the recalcitrant Jews by accommodating himself to their prejudices in order to break them down. As far as we can tell, his only concern was not to get hung up on nonessentials that would take people away from the Christ who had died for them. Furthermore, what John saw in Paul's pastoral practice, he traced back to the teaching of Jesus, who had told his disciples that they would become "fishers of men" (Matt 4:19). As John saw it, the disciples treated their fellow Jews like fish and regarded their message as a hook to ensnare them. Just as real fishermen are patient and wait for the hook to take hold, so the preachers of the gospel persevered with the more obstinate Jews, bowing to their traditions and prejudices when necessary, until such time as the hook could no longer be removed. At that point, so John claimed, the Jews would realize that there was no going back to their former ways and would surrender to the truth of the gospel instead.[12]

What should we make of this? On the one hand, we can agree with John that it is right to approach the task of evangelism with sensitivity and patience, but we recoil from his assertion that this is a form of deception and cannot accept that such behavior would ever be justifiable. To our minds, the disciples of Jesus were not trying to trick Jews into accepting the gospel message but merely trying to avoid unnecessary offense that would put them off hearing it. John saw this as the same technique that adults often use when dealing with recalcitrant children. They get them to lower their guard before springing something on them, hoping all the while that the child's natural resistance will be overcome when he sees that the strange thing that is on offer is not so bad after all. The method is familiar enough, but nowadays we would hesitate to apply it when preaching the gospel to adults. It is only because John believed that in spiritual terms they were *not* adults that he could advocate practices that are essentially immoral, but today it is the principle that adults should be spoken to as adults rather than the idea that the end justifies the means that is more likely to impress us and influence our reaction.

In coming to terms with this we have to reckon with the fact that John was openly anti-Jewish, sometimes stridently so, and he had very little time for the so-called weaker brethren who resisted the truth in the name of their ancient traditions. If Paul accommodated himself to them it was only to reach out to them where they were and make contact. The whole purpose of his ministry to Jews was to make them see things differently—in the light of Christ. As believers progressed from the basics of the gospel to its deeper principles, they would be transformed by the power of the Holy Spirit and abandon beliefs and practices that revealed a childish and immature faith. If they failed to do that, they were not growing in the grace of God, and if they were not growing in grace, then they were not true believers at all. To Chrysostom, this was the fundamental problem with the Jews. They had a revelation suitable to spiritual infants but refused to give it up when a mature, adult faith was revealed in Christ. This refusal showed that they were not true believers, because if they were, they would have responded to the call of the Messiah in the way that Simeon, Anna, and the disciples of Jesus all did.

One feature of accommodation, as John saw it, was its precision. This seems strange at first sight, because no analogy is perfect and therefore it is hard to see how it could be precise or exact. But what John meant by this is that in his revelation, God established specific rules that were quite exact in their formulation and that served to illustrate what he meant by the principles that reflected his character. For example, God is love, a principle that pervades every part of his self-revelation. But what does that mean? Among other things, it means that we do not kill, steal, or commit adultery against our neighbors—these are the practical rules that make it clear how we are to demonstrate what the love of God is. Christian truth is not just a set of principles; it is also a practical program for everyday life. This is why so much of it can only be seen in action. We cannot become like God in his essence, but by the power of the Holy Spirit we can act as God would act in particular circumstances. God loved the world, not by giving it a philosophy to live by, but by sending his Son to die for our salvation. We too are crucified with Christ—united with him in his death and born again with him in his resurrection so that we can now walk in newness of life.

John had a very high view of the Christian life. Origen, who lived about 150 years before him and was the first major Greek-speaking theologian, did not think that it was possible for ordinary people to attain the high spiritual standards demanded of true believers, but John disagreed. He did not believe that spirituality was the preserve of a specially gifted elite, but the inheritance of every Christian. That, of course, merely intensified the need that he felt to expound what the Christian life was and how it should be lived, making his interpretation of the Bible in many respects more "down to earth" and practical than Origen's had been.

It is important to understand this, because in John's time the Greek-speaking world was very much under the spell of Origen and his theology. Origen was struck by how much of the Bible was unacceptable and inapplicable in the literal sense. He could not believe that sin had come into the world in the way that Genesis described it—to him, the story of the serpent and the forbidden fruit was clearly an allegory designed to explain the origin of evil to people who were spiritually incapable of understanding the truth. One way or another, allegory pervades the Scriptures, and it was the duty of the theologian to penetrate behind the veil, as it were, and examine what the unvarnished truth actually was.

In John's day, Origen's propensity for allegory was coming into question and being rejected by many because it often seemed to be fanciful. The great Latin Bible translator Jerome, who was working on his translation at the same time as John was preaching, had initially been enthralled by Origen but turned against him when he realized that allegory was inadequate as a hermeneutic for interpreting the Bible. Many people clung to Origen in spite of this, but John was one of those who had his doubts. Though less emphatic than Jerome, he too abandoned allegory as a general approach to interpretation and began to prefer the literal sense of the text wherever possible. Since Origen and his most dedicated followers were from Alexandria, whereas John and many of those who thought like him were from Antioch, it has become customary to think of this as a rivalry that developed between the two great centers of the Greek-speaking eastern Mediterranean, but this is an exaggeration.

In many ways John was more like an Alexandrian than like the somewhat fictitious "Antiochene school" this scheme has created, and we must be careful not to label him too quickly in this respect. His Christology was certainly closer to that of Alexandria than to what later came to be thought of as Antiochene, and he never went as far in his rejection of allegory as did his contemporary Theodore of Mopsuestia, who was undoubtedly "Antiochene." Given that Theodore was teaching in Antioch when John was preaching there, this difference is important. John rejected allegory, but he adopted something called *theoria*—not "theory" as we think of it now, but something more like "insight" or even "typology." He did not attempt to explain away the literal sense of the biblical text but interpreted it as having a deeper meaning alongside what it said on the surface—the material and the spiritual went together and could not be separated.

This corresponded to John's doctrine of Christ, whom he saw as having two natures (one divine and the other human) but united to such an extent that the human nature never did anything that might distinguish it from the divine. In particular, Jesus was never ignorant of anything, because he was God incarnate, nor was his will distinguishable from that of the Father, despite what he said in the garden of Gethsemane. This was a very different doctrine from that of Theodore, for whom the two natures of Christ were quite separate from one another, but it seems to be virtually identical to the teaching of Athanasius, the great bishop of Alexandria who died a few years before John was ordained. John did not live to see the disruption that would be caused by the struggle to define the nature(s) of the incarnate Christ, and so we cannot say what side he would have been on in those debates. Like Athanasius and Cyril of Alexandria (who lived a generation later than John), he has been claimed by subsequent generations on both sides. It is impossible to rule definitively on this one way or the other, but we who have inherited the "two-natures" Christology of the Council of Chalcedon (held in 451) may sometimes find some of John's language and assumptions uncomfortable, even if we can interpret what he said in ways that cohere with our beliefs today. In that respect, John is a prime example of someone who lived before a particular theological controversy broke out and who was therefore spared the need to decide for one side or the other.

What we can say for certain is that John believed that Jesus Christ was God in human flesh, that everything he thought, said, or did was essentially divine, and that no human being, however gifted or well-intentioned, could rise to Jesus' level. But at the same time, the incarnation of the Son of God was the way in which God accommodated himself to our understanding. What lies beyond our comprehension became visible and tangible, giving us a picture of how we are meant to live. We can never be what Jesus was (and in his resurrection life, still is), but by the indwelling presence of his Holy Spirit we can imitate him, not perhaps in his miracles or teaching, but in his manner of life. As Paul put it, we have the mind of Christ (1 Cor 2:16). He exhorted the Corinthians to imitate him just as he imitated Christ (1 Cor 11:1). In John's view, that meant above all reaching out to others and adjusting to their way of thinking in order to communicate the higher knowledge that comes with the gospel. Just as the Son became a man in order to proclaim salvation to us, so Paul became all things to all people for the same reason and we are called to do the same. The Bible is the blueprint for the life that we are meant to lead, and the preacher is the one who has to adapt its message and apply its teaching to those for whom it is intended.

Central to any preacher's approach to the Bible will be his understanding of how the Old Testament relates to the New (and vice versa), and John was no exception to this. His preference for a literal over an allegorical reading of the Hebrew Bible meant that he had to explain this relationship in a way that took account of history, and he did so by means of what we would now call "promise and fulfillment." More specifically, he used John 4:36–37 to illustrate his point. In those verses Jesus was speaking about the link between the sower and the reaper in the harvest of souls. The reaper is the one who gathers them in, but the sower is glad of this, because his labor has borne fruit. As John saw it, the prophets of the Old Testament were the sowers, and the apostles of the New were the reapers:

The prophets sowed but did not reap; that was the work of the apostles. But even so, the prophets were not deprived of the pleasure and reward of their labors. They rejoice and are glad with us, even though they are not reaping with us. ... I have kept you [Jesus told his disciples] for the work that is less difficult and gives greater joy, for sowing is hard and difficult. ... Jesus was trying to prove that the prophets wanted everyone to come to him. This was also the intention of the law. ... He also showed [his disciples] that he had sent the prophets, and that there is a very intimate connection between the New Testament and the Old.[13]

In following this principle when interpreting the Old Testament, John was doing no more than walking in the footsteps of Jesus, who used the Scriptures for the same purpose. Particularly interesting from our modern point of view is that although John recognized that God had spoken to Israel by more direct means, he pointed out that Jesus did not do the same. He never mentioned the appearance of God to Moses on Mount Sinai, or any of the other Old Testament theophanies. John guessed that the main reason for this reticence was that when those incidents had occurred, many of the people did not believe them or pay any attention to what God was saying. The Scriptures were different in that respect. They were an objective witness to God's revelation that were available to everyone and that Jewish believers deliberately studied in order to discern God's will in them. At the same time, they lacked the discernment they needed in order to understand what the Bible was really all about. The fact that it bore witness to the future coming of Christ was not universally recognized because it was hidden below the surface of the text and had to be deduced by spiritual insight: "When Christ referred the Jews to the Scriptures, he sent them not to a mere reading but to a search. ... The sayings related to him required close attention, for they had been concealed from the beginning ... he therefore asked them to dig down with care in order to discover what lay in the depths below. These sayings were not on the surface, nor were they exposed to open view, but rather lay like buried treasure, hidden very deep."[14]

That they were required to do this was not simply an idea tossed up by Jesus, but something that was rooted in the very identity of Israel. This was why Jesus told the Jews that their human ancestor Abraham had looked forward to his coming (John 8:56), a saying that John interpreted as a reference to the crucifixion, which he saw foreshadowed in the sacrifice that God had first ordered (and then overruled) of his son Isaac.[15] Not surprisingly, it was in this same encounter that Jesus effectively called himself God, by saying, "Before Abraham was, I am" (John 8:58). The revelation of Christ in the Scriptures was ultimately the self-revelation of God to his people, and it was in that combination that the will of God and the fulfillment of his promises to Israel were to be discerned.

CHAPTER 2

In the Beginning

Creation and the Fall

HEAVEN AND EARTH

The most fundamental challenge to the Christian church in the ancient world was its need to convince a pagan culture that the biblical view of creation and the material universe was true. This could only be done by a fundamental restructuring of the concepts of good and evil, because most pagans (in the Roman Empire at least) believed that "spirit" was good and "matter" was evil. The biblical view, in sharp contrast to this, is that all creation is intrinsically good and that evil is the result of a rebellion by spiritual creatures against the rule of God. Nothing in the material universe is naturally evil, though rebellious spirits can (and do) use material things to tempt human beings away from the worship of their Creator. When the first people succumbed to that temptation, sin entered the world, and the entire human race has remained subject to the power of Satan, the leader of the spiritual rebels, ever since. It was to set us free from that bondage and to atone for the sins of humankind against God that the Father sent his Son into the world.

The incarnation of the Son of God as Jesus of Nazareth would not have been possible if matter was irredeemably evil, nor would an experience of salvation in this world have been conceivable. The only way a human being could have escaped from evil would have been by being separated from matter, which is what happens when the soul leaves the body at death. To most pagans, the resurrection of the body was nonsense—why would anyone think that sinful matter ought to be brought back into being? On the other hand, unlike Jews, pagans did not have much trouble believing that a man could become a god—that was a regular occurrence in their mythology and religious practice. Great heroes of the past had been raised to divinity after their death, and the same was true of Roman emperors after they passed away. Nor was the high-minded moral teaching of Jesus particularly objectionable to either Jews or pagans. The details might vary, but there were plenty of prophets and philosophers who taught similar things, and many of them had bands of followers who propagated and refined their beliefs. Nor was anyone particularly surprised by the fact that perfection was unobtainable without considerable suffering and renunciation of the pleasures of this world.

What the ancient Greeks could not fathom was that the world is a coherent universe made by an omniscient, omnipotent Creator who controls its destiny. To Christians, evil was not an unavoidable fact of life but an aberration for which those who were responsible were guilty. Pagans understood that morally good people were sometimes unlucky, and they believed that presumptuous ones would be brought down by their arrogance in trying to defy the inexorable laws of fate, but the idea that everyone is evil, not because of our physical constitution but because of our participation in a universal spiritual rebellion, was beyond their understanding. They lived in fear that forces they could not control were out to get them; the notion of a "personal relationship with God" that could set them free from the power of sin and the fear of destruction did not exist in their minds.

This was why the teaching of Genesis 1–3 was so important for the church. People who did not believe that an originally good world had gone wrong because of the disobedience of spiritual creatures who had been put in charge of it could not understand the gospel of Christ, let alone accept it. Preachers and evangelists all tackled this subject, often more than once. Virtually every theologian from the second to the fifth century wrote about it one way or another. There was a standard literary genre called the *Hexameron* (from the Greek *hexi hēmerai*, meaning "six days") that expounded the biblical doctrine of creation in detail, and several examples of it survive. One of the most famous of them was written by Basil of Caesarea (329?–379). It is a fascinatingly detailed study of biology that demonstrates a degree of scientific knowledge and sophistication that is astonishing for someone who wrote in the premodern era. John did not mention it specifically, but he almost certainly knew of it, and his own exposition of the subject, though much less detailed than Basil's, coheres with his remarkably well.

Other writers, like the great Augustine of Hippo (354–430), who was a contemporary of John's, wrote commentaries on creation—four of them in Augustine's case—that examined the literal (i.e., material) as well as the spiritual sense of the opening chapters of the Bible. John did not know Augustine's works, but his approach was similar.[1] He preached two series of sermons on the subject, one at the very beginning of his career in 386 and the other a year or two later, when he was still in the early stages of his ministry.[2] The first set of eight sermons was short but programmatic for what was to follow; the second was almost identical in content but twice as long.[3] Some scholars have wondered why both series should have come shortly after the launch of his preaching career, but this should cause us no surprise. John knew that if he was to expound the gospel he had to start at the beginning. By choosing to expound Genesis 1–3 he was setting out his own theological principles based on God's self-revelation in Scripture and laying a foundation for his later teaching.

The first point that John made in his exposition was that God speaks to us in ways that we can appreciate. This is the principle of accommodation at its most basic. As he put it, "In the beginning, when God formed human beings, he spoke to them personally, in a way that they could understand."[4] John knew, of course, that the author of the creation narrative, whom he took to be Moses, lived centuries after the events he described and was most unlikely to have heard about them by oral tradition, but that did not lead him to question the truth of the biblical account. On the contrary, John believed that Moses had received his knowledge by direct divine revelation, which made it much more accurate than any tradition could ever be. Moreover, Moses did not waste time on fancy theories or complex introductions to his subject. In the beginning, he said, God created heaven and earth. Everything that now exists, high or low, spiritual or material, was his work. In a simple sentence, the Genesis story undercuts all forms of pagan mythology. There was no primordial conflict between the gods, and no "fall" of spiritual beings into matter. If there was some form of development or evolution, we do not know about it and it does not matter. John understood that these things are beyond our understanding, and he made no attempt to guess what might lie behind the words of the text. What was important to him was not the process but the result—the heaven and the earth that we now live in and experience. In his mind, everything else fits into that framework one way or another.

John recognized that Moses was speaking to Jews, who in his view had a very materialistic approach to life. This was because Jewish laws were very material in their content—what a person ate (or did not eat) was vitally important in determining his standing before God. Later on, the apostle Paul took a different approach when addressing the Athenians, who did not have the same approach to created things that the Jews had. When speaking to them, John said, Paul focused on the futility of pagan worship, arguing that the God who made heaven and earth had no need of temples built with human hands.[5] John's point was that the basic truth of Genesis remains the same but can (and often must) be communicated in different ways, depending on the audience. Once again, we see how John's notion of divine accommodation worked and how he used it in his preaching of the gospel.

John was obviously a creationist, but his approach to the question of origins was more relaxed than what we often find among creationists today. He freely admitted that he was ignorant of the mechanisms that God used to bring the different creatures into being, but was quite firm in stating that no creature, however outlandish or unnecessary it might seem to us, was without purpose or significance in the divine plan. Listen to what he says: "Although you are ignorant of the reason for the existence of created things, do not presume to find fault with their creation. Having heard the Lord give his approval and call them good, how can you be so determined to ask why they were made? Are you deriding their creation as pointless? If you had the right attitude you would be able to discern the power of your Lord and his ineffable love just from their creation."[6]

John did not have to deal with theories of biological evolution, and there is no sign in his writings that he knew anything of that. But he did have to confront people who believed that matter is eternal and that the beings we see around us came into existence more or less spontaneously. Modern skeptics seldom go that far, but the problem John was confronting is just as real today as it was back then. If there is no Creator, where did the world come from and how did it get to be as complex as it is? Can we really believe that such a finely tuned universe has no mind behind it? John thought that such a conclusion was absurd, and in that he was surely right. The Christian claim is easier to believe and makes more sense than any proposed alternative, and that is as true today as it was in John's time.

Perhaps the most interesting thing about John's exposition of Genesis 1 is the fact that he was astute enough to realize that it is not really about creation at all. Creation, he repeatedly states, is fully explained in the first verse. The rest is about how the universe is ordered. There is a progressive series of divine acts that culminate in the creation of humankind, the crowning glory of the world for whom everything on earth was made. It is what we would now call a "big picture" description of material reality, not a detailed analysis of it, which John believed was beyond the capacity of human beings to understand. In the first stage, the world was "invisible and shapeless." Here we come across a textual error that John handled in a very interesting way. By following the general outline of the text as a whole, he was able to arrive at a correct interpretation of the Hebrew original, even though he did not know what that was!

The Hebrew words used here are *tohu wabohu*, an onomatopoeic phrase that means something like "topsy-turvy" and is almost impossible to translate exactly. But the Greek text that John was using made an additional mistake. The usual rendering of *tohu* was *aoristos*, meaning "without boundaries," or "without form," but John's text read *aoratos*, "invisible." In what sense was the original creation invisible? John knew that it could not have been spiritual—the earth was not an angel! It was invisible, not because it was nonmaterial, but because it was covered over by darkness. It was there but could not be seen until the light was brought to bear on it. And of course that is exactly what happened. God said, "Let there be light," and there was light, enough to drive away the darkness and make it possible to discern the contours of the material creation.

It was in the same way that he interpreted the otherwise strange verse that says that "the Spirit of God hovered over the waters." Most people reading this are inclined to think that the Holy Spirit, or perhaps God in his fullness as Spirit, was somehow brooding over the waters, rather in the way that a hen broods over her eggs. But John did not think like that. He supposed that the phrase meant that the waters themselves were teeming with life—the "Spirit of God" was not so much a person of the Trinity as a life force implanted in the waters by God, making it possible for them to breed and to bring forth creatures of many different kinds. As he put it, "What is meant by 'The Spirit of God moved over the water'? I think it means that some life-giving force was present in the waters: the water was not just still and immobile, but moving and possessed of some vital power. What does not move is quite useless, whereas what moves can do many things."[7]

John's interpretation was quite striking for its time, when verses of this kind were regularly used as proofs for Trinitarian theology, which he never mentioned. The theological element came in only when he commented on the next sentence, which is "God separated light from darkness." God brought light into the dark world, but darkness was not expelled from it. Instead, God assigned a place to both light and darkness, recognizing that both had their place in the created order. The triumph of the light was not to be physical but spiritual, and it would not come until the Son of God entered the world. This, said John, was what his namesake the great evangelist meant in the prologue to his Gospel. Jesus Christ was the true light, which enlightens everyone who comes into the world (John 1:9).[8] This light was not intended to make the creation visible but rather to clear our darkened minds from error and point us to the truth. The apostle Paul went a step further when he applied this to the lives of Christians. "Let us walk properly as in the daytime," renouncing the behavior characteristic of those who continue to live in the dark (Rom 13:13).[9]

For John, the sequence here was clear. From the physical creation, which has no moral or spiritual dimension, we proceed first to spiritual understanding and then to moral application. In other words, the Christian life is a spiritual awareness that leads to God-honoring action. Morality without spiritual understanding has no firm basis and is little more than social conformity. Likewise, spiritual knowledge without a resulting change of life is meaningless. As the Protestant Reformers would put it more than a thousand years later, echoing the apostle Paul, "We are saved by grace through faith and not by works, lest anyone should boast" (see Eph 2:8–9). John was not a Protestant, of course, but his understanding of salvation, derived from the apostle Paul, was one that resonated with the Reformers and that continues to be the foundation of our faith and life today.

Along with the separation of light and darkness came the division of the waters into those above the firmament and those below it. Quite what this is supposed to mean has long puzzled commentators. In this respect, John's observations are as pertinent today as they were when first spoken: "What does 'firmament' mean? Is it water that has frozen, air that has been compressed, or something else? No sensible person would be rash enough to pronounce on the matter. It is better just to be grateful and to accept what we have been told, without trying to go beyond the limitations of our nature and inquire into things that are beyond us. It is enough to know the simple fact and to stick to it, which is that the firmament was produced by the Lord's command."[10]

John's commonsense approach left open the question of what exactly the firmament was, but he goes on to note that Genesis says that God called it "heaven." Some people took this to imply that there were different heavens, the one that was originally created and this one, which represented the division of the waters and would more naturally correspond to our word "sky." John rejected this interpretation, saying that there is only one heaven, just as there is only one earth. The firmament is the cosmic order that establishes the difference between these two, and by calling it "heaven" Moses indicated that the former was superior to, and had a controlling influence over, the latter. The entire thrust of the Bible is to raise the sights of people from earth to heaven, not the other way around, and this description of the created order is meant to reinforce that priority.

Oddly enough, this mini-controversy was the occasion for John to discourse more widely on the nature of the Old Testament as a whole. He told his congregation that it was originally written in Hebrew, and that it was at the behest of King Ptolemy II of Egypt, a learned pagan, that it was translated into Greek so that the known world of the time could understand it. He then pointed out that according to the experts, the Hebrew word for "heaven" is plural (*shamayim*), which accounts for the occasional use of the plural in Greek, and that those who spoke Syriac (Aramaic), a closely related Semitic language, confirmed this. The use of the plural was idiomatic and should not be understood numerically, an observation that John believed disposed of the objection to his earlier interpretation. The really strange thing about this, though, is not only that John knew no Hebrew but that he appears to have been ignorant of Syriac as well, even though it was spoken all around him. Furthermore, John gave no indication that he regretted his ignorance; the idea that he ought to learn Hebrew (or Syriac) in order to interpret the biblical text never seems to have crossed his mind.

Here, perhaps more than anywhere else, we can see the great intellectual gulf that separates us from the patristic age. No modern commentator on Genesis would dispense with Hebrew in this fashion, and a command of the original language of the text is essential if we expect to be taken seriously when expounding it. But the ancients believed that all truth is one and that it can be expressed equally well in any language. Bad translations were certainly possible, and John must have known that the Greek Old Testament had been revised several times because of that, but the principle that the message could be expressed just as well in any language remained axiomatic. We disagree with this now, but at the same time we must remember that today virtually all Christians read the Bible in translation and hear it as the Word of God. Reference to the original may sometimes be necessary in order to clarify the meaning, but we continue to believe, as John did, that the essential content can be transmitted accurately in any language, and we expend great effort to demonstrate this by translating the Bible into as many as we can.[11]

Once the firmament was in place, the stage was set for the next act in the drama of creation. The waters below the firmament were gathered together into one place and dry land appeared. This was a logical development in which the original chaos was reduced to order and human life as we know it was made possible. Even today, evolutionary biologists tend to think that life began in the sea and later moved to dry land, so

John's interpretation of the text, though obviously simple, is not incompatible with the most advanced modern science. The key difference is that according to John, it all happened by the command of God. Whatever development (or "evolution") there may have been, it was not spontaneous or haphazard but deliberate and guided by an all-seeing, all-knowing, and perfectly good Creator. John knew nothing about the mechanisms at work (and admitted that he did not understand them), but he was convinced that it was all part of the divine plan for the human race.

The subtext here is that evil is an aberration, a corruption of what God originally intended, and not an intrinsic part of the world order. Because of that, it could be overcome, at least partially, in this life, and would disappear at the end of time, when all things would be made new. Christians are not people trapped in a hostile universe from which there is no escape, but men and women who are full of hope for a future that will be more glorious than anything we now experience, and the fulfillment of what God originally intended for his human creatures. In order to encourage us to think along these lines, John claimed that by saying after each day that God saw what he had made and that it was very good, Moses was telling the people that God was praising his own work. To us this sounds somewhat big-headed, and we would probably not say that about God. But John thought differently. To his mind, if God thought his creation was good enough to praise it, how much more ought we to do the same.[12]

Unfortunately, but not untypically, John used the rhythm of the six individual days of creation to attack Jews. The text says that "evening and morning were one day," and the Jewish calendar began the new day at sundown. No doubt the Genesis account reflected (rather than caused) that practice, but John regarded it as a misinterpretation of Scripture. As he saw it, the evening marked the completion of one day and the morning was the beginning of the next, and he read the account accordingly. It makes little difference in practice, but John evidently found it important enough to use it as a stick to beat the Jews with, which is sad.[13] On the other hand, John had a ready explanation for the fact that Genesis 1 repeats the same phrase after every individual day: "It would have been enough, following all the acts of creation, to say only once that everything God had made was very good, but knowing how limited our minds are, he repeats the process each time, in order to teach us that everything was created with inventive wisdom and ineffable love."[14]

John is at his most interesting when he describes the creation of the sun and moon on the fourth day. He knew what a blessing the sun was and how important it is for human life, but his main concern seems to have been that pagans regularly mistook this and worshiped it instead of the One who had made it. Sun worship, common in antiquity, was for John the supreme manifestation of pagan error in worshiping the creature instead of the Creator. The sun, he claimed, is a bearer of light but not its source, which is why God allowed three whole days to pass before he created it. The same is true of the moon. Though a lesser light than the sun, it serves to illumine the night, making it less dark than it would otherwise be. Both heavenly bodies acted as "signs" because their various phases allowed people to calculate the changing seasons and years. He gives no sign of understanding that the light of the moon is merely a reflection of that of the sun, nor does he say anything about eclipses, probably because they were too rare to have much impact on his congregation. But he was well aware that sailors and others navigate by the sun, moon, and stars, and was quite happy to say that God had put them in heaven for that purpose.[15] Everything in the universe was made for the benefit of humankind, and the sun and moon were no exception to that rule.

John had the somewhat unenviable task of preaching the glories of creation to a congregation that was supposed to be fasting in preparation for Easter. This context is important, and it recurs as a leitmotif in virtually every one of his sermons. For example, he constantly portrays the universe as a great banquet, a feast of delights for the spiritually minded, whose temporary sacrifice of those delights is meant to focus their minds more firmly on the riches of our heavenly Benefactor. Did John succeed in turning his people's minds away from earth to heaven, as he wanted to? It is hard to know for sure, but the evidence of his sermons suggests that this was quite a problem. Some people were evidently fasting, but at the same time they were indulging in other pursuits that were a long way from bringing glory to God: "Let me no longer catch sight of any of you attending race courses, nor spending the best part of the day in unsavory gatherings. Don't spend your time gambling, or in the shouting and brawling that gambling incites. What is the good of fasting if you pass the time playing dice and indulging in mindless nonsense, wasting the whole day in swearing and blaspheming?"[16]

Few pastors today would dare address their audiences quite as forthrightly as this, but perhaps he did not have to worry—many of them were not listening. Few things are more telling than the lament of the preacher who has poured his heart out, but to no avail. John knew what that was like, and felt it deeply, as many of his sermons attest. In his words, "I know that many people are paying no attention to what I am saying. They think it is all stuff and nonsense, and just ignore it. I am sorry about that and regret that there is nothing that can reach people of that kind. ... But I will not stop giving them my advice until I manage to convert them to a better state of mind."[17]

He was true to his word. The seed might all too often have fallen on stony ground, but the sower was called to the task of preaching the word, and John was not the man to shirk it. He may not have been able to reach all those to whom he preached, but his message has echoed down through the ages and brought comfort to many who have found themselves in similar situations. God is always faithful, and even if we do not see the fruit of our labors ourselves, others in due course will, and they will bless God for having sent such bold and fearless messengers to proclaim his gospel.

THE CREATION OF HUMANKIND: PART ONE

Of the seventeen sermons John devoted to Genesis 1–3, no fewer than seven are dedicated to the creation of Adam and Eve, and a further three to their fall from grace and expulsion from the garden of Eden. John was well aware that after seven discourses on the first five days of creation he was moving on to a different and greater subject. On each of the five days, God had issued commands like "Let light be made," or "Let the waters produce reptiles," but on the sixth day his tone changed. In John's words,

> Did you see the whole of creation made in five days merely by word and command? Notice today how great the difference in the wording is. No longer does it say: "Let a human being be created." Instead, it says: "Let us make a human being in our image and likeness." What is new in this? What is strange? Who on earth is this creature whose creation required so much care and planning on the part of the Creator? Do not be surprised … the human being is more important than any other visible beings, and it is for his benefit that all the others have been produced.[18]

But before going on to expound what made Adam unique, John drew the attention of his congregation to something else.

Here for the first time, God speaks in the plural and appears to address his equals in heaven. Adam was to be created "in *our* image and likeness," which to John could only mean that he would be made to resemble both the Father and the Son. To his mind, this was proof that Arianism, the doctrine that said that the Son was a creature inferior to the Father, had to be wrong. Modern commentators generally read this plural as one of majesty, since the word of God in Hebrew is often in the plural form (*Elohim*), but John either did not know that, or if he did, he ignored it.[19] On the other hand, he rightly understood that the "image" did not refer to Adam's form but rather to the authority that was to be given to him, to exercise dominion over the rest of the material creation.[20]

John justified this interpretation in two ways. First of all, he said that the verses in question (Gen 1:26-27) were followed immediately by the divine command to rule over the earth, making it obvious that that is what the "image" referred to. Second, he used the apostle Paul's description of the same thing in 1 Corinthians 11:7, where Paul distinguishes between Adam, who was created in the image of God, and Eve, who was made in the image of Adam, as proof that authority must be what was meant, because Adam and Eve were equal in "form" (i.e., species) but Eve was subordinate to Adam in terms of authority. If "image" in Genesis 1:26-27 was a generic term referring to humanity, Paul's argument would have made no sense, since at that level Adam and Eve are equal.[21] John's interpretation was unusual in his day, since most of his contemporaries believed that "image" should be understood in terms of being, rather than of function, but modern research has confirmed his understanding. On the other hand, like most Greeks, he did not perceive that "likeness" was just a synonym for "image" but thought that it was something in addition to it. He said that we are meant to resemble God in our gentleness, mildness, and virtue, following Jesus' command to be like our Father in heaven.[22] It is therefore easy to see why he believed that by falling away from God, Adam and Eve lost the likeness but retained the image—human beings still have authority over the rest of creation, but they no longer resemble their Creator in the way that they were originally meant to do.

It is common nowadays to criticize men like John for their apparent sexism in denying the complete equality of male and female, but this is a misunderstanding. John most emphatically did *not* deny that—on the contrary, he affirmed it quite specifically. But alongside this fundamental equality there was a diversity of roles that gave a certain primacy to the male. As John understood it, this primacy could be compared to the relationship between the Father and the Son, both of whom were equal, but who related to each other in the way that the names given to them suggest. It is the Son who does the will of his Father, not the other way round, just as it is Adam who is the head of Eve, and not the reverse.

Never one to pass up an opportunity for practical application, John goes on to tell his hearers that they must not only share his message with others, but also practice what they preach. He does not dwell on female submission to the male, as we might expect, but on the true meaning of fasting. We are reminded here that these sermons were preached in Lent, when fasting was enjoined on the church, and John wasted no time in telling people that "the person fasting ought above all to keep anger in check, learn the lesson of mildness and kindness, have a contrite heart, banish the flood of unworthy passions." That was real fasting.[23] A modern reader might regard this as a digression from the main subject, and perhaps it is, but John did not see it that way. What he wanted to communicate to his people was that individual self-discipline and the practice of virtuous living were the essential foundations for all relationships. Human beings cannot act as the image of God if they are not properly reflecting his standards, and that must be the fundamental principle governing how male and female interact with each other—not domination, but authority and obedience in mutual love.

Throughout this series of sermons, John never let his hearers forget the importance and significance of fasting, which to his mind was the seedbed of all virtue. For example, he said that we must "keep tight control over our reasoning and have a humble opinion of ourselves," because if we do that, "we will be able to pray with a clear mind and obtain God's grace by confessing our sins."[24] Later on, he took his congregation to task because some of them were too busy eating to come to church. He did not insist that they fast beforehand, but challenged them to get things in their proper balance. He thought that spiritually minded people ought to be able to eat without losing their appetite for God's word. As he put it, "The shameful thing is not coming to this spiritual teaching after eating, but coming with an attitude of sloth, an addiction to passion and a failure to control body movements. There is nothing wrong with eating; the harmful thing is gluttony … which destroys even the pleasure that comes from food. Likewise, there is nothing wrong with drinking in moderation, but only with drunkenness and a loss of self-control through excess."[25]

John was not a legalist, even in Lent. He always reminded people that self-discipline had a higher purpose and should be practiced for the benefits it brings and not out of a sense of obligation only. He was quite clear about this when he advised people whose poor health did not allow them to fast to eat as necessary but in so doing to show even greater zeal for spiritual things.[26]

Returning to the theme of dominion over the creation, John found himself having to deal with what to us seems like a strange objection. Pagans, it seems, criticized the Christian claim on the ground that we do not control the wild beasts. John's retort was simply that "whenever a human being appears, wild animals flee." If they attack us because they are hungry (for example), this is not because they have some control over us, but because we have disturbed or mistreated them in some way.[27] But John's real concern was to relate the wild beasts to the disordered desires of our own minds. As John put it, animals behave according to their natures—some are tame and others are savage. But human beings go against their natures by entertaining ferocious thoughts that we ought not to have. Our failure to tame them and behave in a way that glorifies God is an aberration that condemns us. As John put it, lions are wild beasts deprived of reason, but human beings are rational and ought to have the fear of God present in them.[28]

The supreme example of how much the fall of humankind has changed the created order can be seen from the way in which Eve conversed with the serpent in the garden of Eden. Had she already fallen from grace, she would have run away from such a dangerous animal, just as we do now. But because the wild beasts were still subject to human authority, Eve had no fear of them and was quite prepared to enter into conversation with the serpent.[29] Our fear of snakes comes from the loss of our authority over them that is the result of the fall; we can no longer control what we were originally meant to have dominion over. This explanation will strike most modern readers as somewhat odd, but it makes sense from John's point of view and can fairly claim to be a biblical perspective, at least in the sense that hostility between human and beast (and between different animals) does appear to be one of the effects of the fall.

In this respect, John's take on the way human beings and animals relate to one another seems curious to us but was understood by him to be an example of God's mercy to fallen humanity. As he said, "Adam broke the entire commandment and the law, but God, in his lovingkindness, showed that his goodness is superior to human transgressions, and did not completely remove our honor and authority. Instead, he withdrew from our control only those animals which are of no use to us, leaving the others under our authority and dominion. He left herds of cattle for plowing, beasts of burden for transport and flocks of sheep to provide [wool for] clothing."[30]

Fanciful John's interpretation may well be, but at least he makes the important point that God did not abandon Adam to his fate. We may want to describe his mercy toward us in somewhat different terms, but the principle is surely the same for us now as it was for him back then. Perhaps the most remarkable thing about this is that the dominion that God originally gave to Adam was extended to Eve and to their posterity as well. John is particularly eager to establish that Eve would share in Adam's tasks, and that God made that clear even before she was created.[31] Today, most of us would probably not notice this detail, but to John it was very important, and we must draw attention to it so as to avoid any suggestion that he was sexist in his approach. Eve might be expected to defer to the authority of her husband, but when it came to the rest of creation she was given exactly the same privileges as Adam had. In a world where many people were inclined to think that women were inferior to men, not only socially but in their very being, this assertion struck an important blow for what we would now call "women's rights" and it is incumbent on us to recognize that fact. John would have had less trouble integrating into our modern world than many of his contemporaries or successors would have had, and this is all because he stuck closely to the literal meaning of the biblical text and was not tempted to read it through the lens of ancient misogyny.

Having completed the creation in six days, God rested on the seventh, the Genesis account tells us. Explaining this was a challenge for John. First of all, it might suggest that God has now gone into retirement, and that Christians ought to follow him in doing nothing. Second, it might be understood as contradicting Jesus' claim that both he and the Father were still at work (John 5:17). To avoid such misinterpretations, John was careful to state that the seventh day has its own special characteristics. Each of the other days was dedicated to one aspect of creation or another, but the seventh day was dedicated to God. By blessing it and sanctifying it, "God provides us with instruction in a cryptic manner, teaching us that he set aside the whole of one day in the cycle of the week and marked it off for the performance of spiritual works."[32] Rest, in John's eyes, was purely relative; it was not laziness, but a pause in the normal course of life in order to give glory to God and to reflect more deeply on his love and provision for us. Far from being an escape from our responsibilities, it was an occasion for fulfilling them. In a world where leisure was rare and people spent a great deal of time just trying to survive, the day of rest and the provision of the night for sleeping were signs of God's mercy toward us. In John's words, "Just as unremitting tension leads to exhaustion ... so too, constant resting produces laziness. This happens to both the soul and the body. This is why moderation in all things is the best way."[33]

Later on he would go into this more deeply, by reminding his hearers that God put Adam in the garden of Eden, not so that he could pass his days in idleness, living off the fruit of the land, but so that he could till the soil and watch over it.[34] There was pleasure in work and satisfaction in seeing it well done. In the garden, Adam would not be impeded by weeds, stones, and other things that get in the way of the farmer's earthly labors since the fall, but work itself was sanctified and part of God's original purpose for humankind.

THE CREATION OF HUMANKIND: PART TWO

Interpreters have long recognized that Genesis 2:4-25 contains a different account of creation from the one that precedes it. Modern scholars have tended to say that it represents an alternative creation narrative that was added to the other one at some point in the redaction process that produced Genesis as we know it, but John had a different interpretation. To him, the earlier narrative was a survey of the six stages by which creation was ordered. The second narrative takes all that for granted and concentrates instead on certain points that were glossed over in the first chapter. This was sound pedagogical method—start with the basic framework and then fill in the details, concentrating on what is really important. What mattered to John was that human beings, made in the image of God, were also formed from the dust of the earth. John insisted that we have been made, not out of the finest topsoil, but from the lowest form of dust—there is no room for pride or arrogance in our relationship either to God or to the rest of the universe. We have nothing to boast about, and everything we have and are is a gift of God.[35]

John also placed great emphasis on the fact that God breathed into the body that he had formed from the dust, and Adam became a living soul. The soul is thus the life force of the body, and without it, the flesh is nothing at all. Here we see that John betrayed a Greek tendency to analyze the concept of "flesh" in a way that does not do justice to the biblical meaning of the term. To him, it was the inert corpse that nevertheless has desires that drag down the soul, which has given it life. That is a form of Platonism, the idea that the human being is a soul imprisoned in a body, and like most of his contemporaries John simply assumed that it is what the Bible taught. This led him to say things like the following: "Realizing the nobility of our soul, let us not be guilty of any behavior that is unworthy of it, nor defile it with unfitting actions, subjecting it to the thrall of the flesh and showing so little appreciation and regard for what is so noble and endowed with such preeminence."[36]

John's inability to see that flesh and soul together constitute a spiritual reality that is now in rebellion against God, and that it is not possible to separate a "good" soul from an "evil" body of flesh, compromises much of what he has to say about living the Christian life. But it is only fair to add that this misunderstanding was shared not only by his contemporaries but by most of his successors down to the time of the Reformation; it is by no means absent even now. He was wrong, but he was in good company, and we must bear that in mind when we assess his legacy and its influence. On a more positive note, John saw that the remedy for the soul's plight could only come from the Bible, which had been given to God's people for that purpose: "Our loving Lord, knowing the weakness of our intentions and our tendency to fall, has left us great remedies in the reading of the Scriptures so that we might constantly apply them to ourselves and recall the lives of those great and wonderful men [mentioned in them]."[37] John's understanding of human nature may have been faulty, but at least he knew that something has gone wrong, and more importantly, he also knew where to go to find the answers that we need to put matters right.

One point that John makes about the creation of Adam is that it was not "out of nothing" (*ex nihilo*) in the way that everything else was, but out of preexisting dust. Adam was therefore not independent of the rest of creation but an integral part of it, and his soul was the God-breathed force that gave it life. John had to say this in order to counter the common pagan belief that human souls were elements of the divine that had somehow fallen into matter and been captured by it. On the contrary, the soul was a gift given to the body that had already been formed from the dust. It is superior to the flesh, to be sure, but not independent of it. John did not say so at this point, but it is because of this that Christians believe in the resurrection of the body, and not in mere soul survival after death. That belief is a direct contradiction of Platonism and must be taken into account when trying to decide how great its influence on John and his contemporaries actually was.

Having discussed the mechanics of the creation of humanity at great length, John followed the biblical narrative by going on to describe the garden of Eden, which like humankind itself was not created independently but rather set aside as a special place in the already existing world. In a further blow to the Platonic worldview, John believed that it was essential to point out that the garden was on earth, and did not represent some heavenly state. In other words, the fall of Adam was *not* from heaven (the spiritual realm) to earth (the material world) but a spiritual disobedience to God's commands that took place *within* the physical universe.[38] Perhaps because of his insistence on the materiality of the garden, John went on to say that God created two trees, distinct from those in the rest of the world, that he planted in it. One of these was the tree of life, and the other was the tree of the knowledge of good and evil.[39] He did not dwell on them at length, which is surprising, but the explanation may be that he had fallen into an embarrassing trap that he did not know how to escape from, and so he passed over it as quickly as possible. The names of the trees indicate that they are not to be interpreted literally, but John had painted himself into a corner here and saw no immediate way out of it.[40]

One important feature of the more detailed narrative of the creation of human beings is that God prepared everything for Adam alone. It was only when the garden was complete and he was installed in it that he saw the need for human companionship, and it was at that point that he created woman. Once again, just as Adam was formed from preexisting matter, so the woman was taken out of the man's side, a feature which shows us that she is fully equal to him and yet dependent on him at the same time.[41] It was only after the appearance of the woman that Adam began to exercise his dominion over the rest of the creation, a sign that his authority was to be exercised in common with her. She was not to be dominated or controlled in the way that the animals were, but rather to share in his rule as one who was just as rational and capable as he was.[42]

In describing the way in which the woman was formed, John showed a dexterity that somehow escaped him when he was describing the two trees in the garden. He knew perfectly well that God did not literally take one of Adam's ribs and make a woman out of it, but he insisted that the Bible uses this imagery for a particular purpose. As he explained to his congregation: "Do not take these words literally, but interpret the concreteness of the expressions from the standpoint of human limitations. If God had not used these words, how would we have been able to understand mysteries that defy description? Let us therefore not remain at the level of the words alone, but understand everything in a way that is proper to God because it is spoken of him."[43]

John went on to give great emphasis to what Adam said when he saw the woman whom God had provided for him. She was bone of his bones, and flesh of his flesh, and therefore essentially the same as he was (Gen 2:23). John also picked up what the apostle Paul had to say about this. Paul taught that woman comes from man, making an order in their relationship, but he also added that man is not independent of woman, and that they need each other to fulfill God's purpose (1 Cor 11:8–11). John made much of the fact that a man was to leave his parents and cling to his wife once he got married. This seems fairly obvious to us today, but in the ancient world it was not so. Family ties were vertical more than horizontal, and no man would lightly disregard his parents (and particularly not his father) because of his wife. Yet John was not afraid to challenge this pattern on the basis of biblical teaching, and in so doing he laid the foundations for a transformation of the nature of the family as it was then understood. Change did not come overnight, of course, but the seeds were sown in the Scriptures and the preaching of a man like John brought that home to the Christian community.

At this point, alas, John relapsed into the prejudices of his time. Following the text of Scripture, he noted that Adam and his wife were "naked but not ashamed" because they did not know what nakedness was. According to John, they were covered with the glory of God, which is what they saw when they looked at one another, and not bare flesh. In line with this, however, John also claimed that human intercourse leading to procreation began only after the fall, the assumption being that if they had not listened to Satan and disobeyed God, they would not have had sexual relations or produced children. John did not notice that such an interpretation was in complete contrast to God's command in Genesis 1:28, where he told them to "be fruitful and multiply." It may be true that this did not begin until after the fall, but that was probably because if it had, the children produced in the garden would presumably not have been subject to the punishment meted out to the parents. That is speculation, of course, but we are at least entitled to say that sexual intercourse was not the result of the fall—an error that was widely shared in ancient times (and since) and that has done enormous harm to the church over the centuries.

The insidiousness of this can be seen most clearly some time later, when John returned to the subject and examined it in greater detail. Not only did sexual intercourse not begin until after the fall, but in the garden they practiced the higher life of virginity. The monastic life that was then in full bloom, and the centuries of confusion over the value of sexual intercourse that were to follow, lasting in some quarters up to the present time, are eerily foreshadowed in John's account of the creation: "At the outset and from the beginning the practice of virginity was in force, but when, through their indifference, disobedience entered the scene and the way of sin was opened, virginity disappeared because they had proved themselves to be unworthy of such a good thing. ... How great is virginity therefore, how elevated and important it is, because it surpasses nature and requires assistance from on high."[44]

John also claimed that Adam and his wife "were living like angels in paradise and therefore not burning with desire, nor assaulted by other passions, nor subject to the needs of nature, but incorruptible and immortal, so for that reason alone they had no need to wear clothes."[45] Unfortunately, there is no evidence to support these somewhat extravagant claims, and to say that they were living in an angelic state seems to contradict the fact that they were on earth and not in heaven. There is an inconsistency here, but it was one that John insisted on and that, in his mind at least, even helped to explain the fall, as we shall see. John also believed that when God said that if Adam ate of the tree of the knowledge of good and evil, he would surely die, what he meant was that Adam would lose his immortality and become subject to death. In a sense, that was true because neither Adam nor Eve was struck dead when they ate the forbidden fruit, but the text seems to imply that when that happened, their protection against death was taken away, not that they became mortal when previously they had not been.[46]

Having dealt with the various details of the creation of humankind, John went on to describe the nature of their fall from grace, and here he was on surer ground. Whatever we think about the original creation, we have to admit that much of it is necessarily hypothetical. We cannot say what would have happened if the fall had not occurred for the simple reason that it did, and we are now stuck with the consequences. John obviously felt more comfortable in dealing with actual realities rather than with theoretical possibilities, and in this respect he showed a sure theological and pastoral instinct. Unlike a philosopher, the pastor and preacher has to deal with what is, not with what he would like to see, and it is with some relief that we can turn from the realm of ideas back to the context of practical application that John's sermons are so noted for. Theories come and go, but pastoral realities remain much the same down through the ages and across cultures, and it was to them that John now turned his attention.

THE FALL OF ADAM AND EVE

In treating the fall of Adam and Eve, John left his hearers in no doubt as to the true origin of evil. It was not Adam's disobedience that lay at its root, but rather the rebellion of Satan, an angel who had tried to make himself equal with God. According to John, Satan attacked our first parents because he thought they were similar to him and saw no reason why they should enjoy such blessings in the garden of Eden. In his words, "The author of evil, seeing an angel who happened to live on earth, was consumed by envy, since he himself had once enjoyed a place among the powers above, but had been cast down from that pinnacle because of the depravity of his will and exceeding wickedness."[47]

John's approach to the serpent in the garden was simply to say that Satan found the serpent and took it over as a useful means of achieving his end: "[Satan] discovered this wild animal, the serpent, overcoming the other animals by his cunning. ... He made use of this creature as an instrument and through it deceived the naive and weaker vessel, namely, woman, by means of conversation."[48]

John avoided saying that Satan and the serpent were the same, and he certainly did not think that this particular serpent had been specially created for the purpose of deceiving Eve. The physical serpent was simply the means to achieve a malign spiritual end and was punished for his part in Satan's schemes. Eve, on the other hand, was guilty not only of responding to Satan's temptation but also of divulging God's will to him. God had told Adam and Eve not to eat of the tree and John seems to have thought that Satan did not know that. As he put it, "Through her grave negligence she not only failed to turn away [from Satan] but revealed the whole secret of the Lord's direction, thus casting pearls before swine. ... She exposed to swine, that is to the evil beast through whom the devil was acting, the divine pearls. He not only trampled on them and opposed them with his words, but turned and led into disobedience not only her but also the first-formed man with her."[49]

As so often, John did not hesitate to apply Eve's experience to believers today. The swine before whom the divine pearls were cast were no more real swine than the pearls were real pearls—we are talking here about divine sayings being wasted on people who behave like swine. The lesson, said John, is that we must take care not to share the mysteries of God with those who are incapable of receiving them, because if we do they are liable to turn against us and bring on us the same fate as befell Adam and Eve.

John was fully aware of the nature of Satan's temptation, and here again he used it as a lesson for us. In order to seduce Eve, he promised her something wonderful—equality with God—but that was both beyond his power to grant and beyond her ability to receive. As John described it, "Not content to remain within her own proper limits, but considering the enemy and foe of her salvation to be more trustworthy than God's words, [Eve] learned shortly afterward through her own experience the lethal effect of such advice and the disaster brought on them from tasting the fruit."[50]

The message could not have been clearer. Behave like Eve, and we too will suffer the consequences. It was customary in ancient times to blame Eve for the fall, but although John could hardly avoid her responsibility, he did not on that account exonerate Adam. On the contrary, Adam should have known better than to listen to Eve, and his failure to exercise his responsibility toward her led them both into disaster.[51] As John told his congregation, "Put the blame on no one but yourself and your own neglect; after all, if you had not been willing, your wife would have been unable to bring you to this disastrous state."[52]

The fall into sin removed the glory of God that had enveloped the first couple, and it was then that they recognized that they were naked because they were no longer protected. Commenting on the fact that they stitched together fig leaves and made themselves skirts, John said, "This is what you get by following the devil's deceit. Not only does he fail to improve our benefits but he leaves us naked and bereft of those we already have."[53] Later on, he added that God made clothes out of skins for them to wear, replacing his glory with the rough-hewn garments of slaves, but nevertheless preserving them and protecting them from the self-destruction they had otherwise brought on themselves.[54]

At this point, John returned to the question of the tree of the knowledge of good and evil, and it seems that he had regained the composure that evidently escaped him when he first mentioned it. He still maintained that it was a real tree, but not that it was of some special type. As he put it, "It was not because it supplied the knowledge [of good and evil] that the tree was so called, but because the transgression of the command happened to concern the tree. From that event, knowledge of sin entered the world, and that is why the tree got the name that it did."[55]

An ordinary tree, in other words, that was used for an extraordinary purpose, rather in the way that the serpent was an ordinary animal commandeered for a particular task. In both cases, John managed to combine what seemed perfectly natural on the surface with the playing out of a cosmic drama that would otherwise be almost impossible for a human mind to grasp.

Later on, when dealing with the tree of life from which Adam and Eve were cut off, John explained this as an act of divine mercy. As he saw it, if the couple had eaten the fruit of that tree they would live, and go on sinning forever, with no hope of redemption through death and resurrection. Expelling them from the garden and blocking their access to the tree was therefore an act of divine compassion, and not the punishment that the undiscerning would most probably assume it to have been.[56]

The discovery of Adam and Eve's disobedience did not take long. The Bible describes God strolling in the garden in the evening, and says that the two humans did what they could to hide from him. Obviously the story is symbolic, but John realized that it corresponds to the psychology of sin and expounded it accordingly. Adam was afraid of meeting God because his conscience accused him of having transgressed the divine law.[57] John knew the power of conscience, and the need to hide from wrongdoing. It is particularly interesting to see how he dealt with God's response to Adam's failure. Instead of condemning him outright, God goes looking for him and asks leading questions, hoping to tease out of Adam himself a confession of what he had done. Adam was given every chance to explain himself and to confess of his own free will. God was not primarily interested in punishing him, but rather he wanted to restore Adam to health if that was at all possible. As always, God's behavior is meant to set us an example: "God teaches us through this that when we judge the guilty, we should not berate them harshly or display the savagery of wild beasts toward them, but employ as much long-suffering and mercy as we can, because we are dispensing justice to our fellows, and out of a sense of kinship with them we should temper justice with love."[58]

On the other hand, when dealing with the serpent and his master Satan, God did not hesitate to condemn them out of hand. The deceivers were much guiltier than the deceived, and so the forbearance shown to Adam and Eve was denied them. John understood that there are degrees of guilt and therefore degrees of punishment; those who are trapped into doing something wrong are not as responsible as those who set the trap for them, even though neither is innocent. John further knew that while God was even then preparing a way of salvation for Adam and Eve, that rescue would not be available to the perpetrators of the evil, who were forever condemned. Yet another lesson for us to learn, for if we follow the way of the serpent we shall be shown no mercy, whereas if we repent and turn away from our sins, we shall be delivered from them, even if there are some ways in which we shall have to suffer the consequences of our actions.[59]

For the woman, the consequence would be pain and suffering in childbirth, but that would be compensated for by the joy of seeing a new child born. John lived in a world where there were no anesthetics and where the risks in having children could be very great, but he knew that women were not put off by the dangers they faced. Even when a mother dies in the course of giving birth, other women are not put off and continue to long for children, so great is the recompense for the suffering they have to endure.[60] For the man, the punishment was that he would have to work hard to till the soil, which was cursed because of his sin. But John notes that there is a big difference between what happened to the serpent and what happened to Adam. In the first case, it was the serpent itself that was cursed, but in the second it was the ground, not the man. God's judgment may seem harsh at first sight, but in reality it is much more lenient than what he meted out to those whose sin was effectively unforgivable.

CHAPTER 3

John's Portrait of Jesus

HIS APPROACH TO THE SOURCE MATERIAL

Like all Christians, John's eyes were firmly focused on Jesus Christ, the Son of God, who became a man, who died for our sins, and who rose again to give us new and eternal life in him. The central message of the gospel was never far from his mind, and it comes out in numerous ways throughout his preaching career. But in addition to that, John has left us two full-length series of ninety sermons on the Gospel of Matthew and eighty-eight on the Gospel of John, which analyze the source material for the earthly life of the Savior in greater depth and consistency. The series on Matthew stands out because it is the only complete one on that Gospel that we possess from the ancient world. The sermons on John have parallels elsewhere, not least in the *Tractates on the Fourth Gospel* that come from the pen of John's great contemporary Augustine, but they too bear the stamp of Chrysostom's particular outlook and are of great importance for understanding how he understood the message and earthly ministry of Jesus.

As far as the historical details of Jesus' life are concerned, John's sermons are bound to be somewhat disappointing to modern readers. We have to remember that he lived more than 350 years after the events described in the Gospels, and although some things had not changed in the interval, much had, and John was no better informed about first-century Palestine than most of us are about seventeenth-century England. The Roman Empire was still in place, and the Greek language was just as widely used in John's day as it had been in Jesus'; but the Jewish world that we meet in the New Testament had long since disappeared. There was no temple in Jerusalem, and there were no Pharisees either. The Jews of John's day had clearly rejected Jesus as their Messiah, and the lines between them and Christians were much more firmly drawn than they had been in New Testament times. In John's homilies, this sense of distance and alienation between Jews and Christians is inescapable, and it inevitably colors his approach, often in ways that make people today, who are aware of the centuries of persecution that Jews were later to suffer, especially uncomfortable.

John's access to the life and times of Jesus was primarily literary—he had no sense of archaeology and never thought to consult historical archives, even if they were available (which is by no means certain). He knew that the first three Gospels were too similar in structure and content to be completely independent of one another, and in a sense he can be said to have addressed what modern scholars know as the "Synoptic problem": How did these Gospels come into being, and why are there three of them and not just one? To this question John would have added the Fourth Gospel, which, although it was clearly different from the other three, was nevertheless part of a wider pattern of Gospel writing.

John believed that Matthew, the disciple of Jesus, was the author of the First Gospel, and he was particularly struck by the fact that God would entrust such a task to someone as morally suspect as a tax collector. From John's point of view, that demonstrated how great was the transforming power of God, who could take a sinner like Matthew and make him the first (and in some ways greatest) of the evangelists.[1] John was struck by the way in which Jesus condescended to call people from the lowliest and least-regarded occupations and turn them into his disciples and future apostles. In his sermons on the Fourth Gospel he pointed out at some length how remarkable the calling of John the Evangelist was: "From what country did he come? From no country, but from a poor village and from a land little esteemed that produced nothing of any value. ... His father was a poor fisherman, so poor that he took his sons into the same line of work. ... As for education, he had none."[2]

John further believed that Matthew had written his account, not of his own volition, but because some Jewish Christians had asked him to do it, and that he had composed his text in their native language.[3] He immediately added that Mark had done the same thing, but not Luke, who was addressing a wider audience. As evidence for this, John cited the genealogy of Jesus given in Matthew, which is structured in covenant terms and stretches back no further than Abraham, and contrasted it with Luke's version, which takes the human ancestry of Jesus all the way back to Adam.

John appreciated the artificial structure of Matthew's genealogy of Jesus, which forced the account into three sections of fourteen generations each, with the last falling short by a generation. He was also sensitive to the fact that while the Babylonian captivity plays an important part in the selection, the time of slavery in Egypt is not mentioned at all. John explained this apparent oddity as follows: "[The Israelites] had ceased to be afraid of the Egyptians, but not of the Babylonians. Egyptian slavery was ancient, but the Babylonian captivity was still fresh in their minds. And besides, the people did not go to Egypt because of any sins they had committed, but they were taken away to Babylon on account of their transgressions."[4] There was a spiritual lesson to be learned from the exile that did not apply to the descent into Egypt, and John believed that it was for that reason that Matthew's genealogy was composed in the way it was. In seeking to explain why there are four Gospels instead of only one, John made his appeal to the greater reliability that he believed attached to the number of witnesses: "One [evangelist] would have been enough, but if there are four that write, not at the same time or in the same place, nor after consultation with each other, but still speak as if from a single mouth, this becomes very serious evidence for the truth [of what they say]."[5]

At the same time, John was also aware that there were discrepancies in their accounts that had to be explained, and he promised his hearers that he would rise to the occasion. As he told them, "These discrepancies are very great evidence of their truth. If they had agreed about everything completely and in exactly the same words, our enemies would have been convinced that they had conspired together to achieve this, because such total agreement does not come about naturally. But the slight disparities that exist in secondary matters free them from all such suspicion and speak volumes in favor of the writers' character. Minor differences relating to such matters as time and place do not compromise the overall truth of what they said."[6]

Of course, when it came to offering solutions to such problems John could only speculate, and readers must judge for themselves how plausible his explanations are. Suffice it to say that his overall point remains valid. The evangelists did not collude with each other to provide a common account, the points on which they differ are almost all immaterial as far as the main argument is concerned, and the story they tell has the ring of truth. No two people perceive events in exactly the same way, and what to us may seem puzzling can easily represent different perspectives that could be harmonized if we knew all the facts.

John rounded off his discussion by pointing his hearers to the common ground that all the evangelists shared. God had become a man, he performed miracles, he was crucified and buried, he rose again and ascended into heaven, and he will come back as judge. In his teaching, he gave commandments that point to the way of salvation, he expounded a new law that supplemented but did not contradict the Old Testament, and he revealed that he was the true and only-begotten Son, consubstantial with the Father. In these things we can hear echoes of the great creeds, though the order in which John presents his material suggests that he was not actually quoting any one of them. What we have here is testimony to the mindset of the age that composed texts like the so-called Nicene Creed, that outline what people of that time regarded as fundamental to the proclamation of the gospel.[7]

Like most of his contemporaries, John believed that Matthew's Gospel was the earliest to have been written, which is why it is placed first in the New Testament. He saw Mark as a kind of abbreviated version, and Luke as an account adapted to further the gentile mission of Paul. Most likely he saw no need to comment on either of them specifically, but he did not hesitate to draw on them in the course of his exposition of Matthew. He even expressed the view that Matthew's Gospel is a kind of golden mean between Mark and Luke, who represented the voices of Peter and Paul respectively. Paul, in John's eyes, was a mighty orator who discoursed at some length, whereas Peter was the soul of brevity, a contrast between them that the two Gospels reflect. There may well be something in the view that Mark reflects Peter whereas Luke is closely tied to Paul, but whether this explains their relative length is more questionable. John never said it directly, but it seems likely that he chose to expound Matthew and John, rather than Mark or Luke, because in his eyes they were both written by eyewitnesses of the events they describe, whereas the others were not. This makes perfect sense from his point of view and demonstrates that John had a critical awareness of his material that would not go amiss today, though of course modern scholars do not share his presuppositions about the authorship of the Gospels in question.

One point raised by Matthew's Gospel is the question of the reliability of the Septuagint (LXX) translation of the Old Testament. This is of particular relevance because of the prophecy in Isaiah 7:14 regarding the birth of the Messiah, which is quoted in Matthew 1:23. The LXX translated "a virgin shall conceive," but John was aware that later Greek translations, which aimed for greater accuracy, put "young woman" instead of "virgin," and that this called the authenticity both of Matthew and of the prophecy into question. John's answer to this was exemplary and can still be found in commentaries today. First of all, he argued (correctly) that the LXX predated the coming of Christ, whereas the "corrected" versions did not. John suggested that the later translators deliberately chose "young woman" in order to discredit the Christian claim about Mary's virginity, which is possible, even if perhaps not as likely as he thought. John also knew that the term "young woman" was sometimes used in the Old Testament to mean "virgin," since the definition of "youth" was bound up with lack of sexual experience. Finally, and this is perhaps his strongest point, he argued that a sign must be something special, and there was nothing special about a young woman giving birth. The gist of the passage, in both Isaiah and Matthew, supports the translation "virgin," regardless of the actual word used.[8] Some modern scholars might find John's claims somewhat forced and reject them, but there can be no doubt that he was aware of the issues at stake and that his reaction showed a degree of sophistication that would not be out of place today.

John did not address the question of the census that took place in the reign of Augustus and that has caused so much argument in modern times (see Luke 2:1).[9] But he did consider the star that appeared in the East and the wise men ("magi") who traveled to Jerusalem, looking for the newly born "king of the Jews." He believed that the star was something out of the ordinary, even to the point of suggesting that it was a star in appearance only—in reality, he thought, it was a special power that did not behave as an ordinary star would. He justified this view by pointing out that the so-called star was able to pinpoint a manger in Bethlehem, a degree of precision that would normally escape a heavenly body of that kind.[10] As to why God would have acted in that way, John was quite clear—it was in order to rebuke the unbelief of the Jews. For centuries, prophets had predicted the coming of the Messiah, but nobody listened, and they did not recognize him when he appeared. Yet Persian wise men immediately realized that something extraordinary had occurred, even though they were ignorant of the details. John saw this as fulfilling what Jesus said to his disciples, when he told them that the "men of Nineveh" would rise up and condemn the Jews on the day of judgment, as would the queen of Sheba (Matt 12:41–42).[11] In John's day, as in Jesus', Nineveh was part of the Persian Empire and could plausibly be regarded as the home of the magi, even though they were more likely to have come from Babylon.

To the objection that God should not have used a pagan pseudo-science like astrology in order to proclaim the coming of his Son into the world, John had a simple reply. What else could he have done? The magi would not have listened to the prophets, of whom they had no knowledge. God had to meet them where they were, since otherwise they would not have understood the message being communicated to them. In support of this, he quoted Paul's use of the pagan poets when addressing the men of Athens, who would not have understood an argument drawn from the Hebrew Bible (Acts 17:23, 28). This explanation was fully in line with John's general approach, and it needs to be appreciated as such. People have to be met with the gospel message where they are and in a way that is accessible to them, since otherwise they cannot hear it. That does not justify the general use of the means adopted in particular cases—the fact that the magi responded to an astrological appeal is not a recommendation of astrology as a means of predicting the future, or for anything else. John pointed out that the magi did not get the whole message from the star—they were guided to Jerusalem and there directed to the scribes of the temple, who pointed them to the specific prophecy in Micah 5:2, which said that the Messiah would be born in Bethlehem.[12] The lesson was that both Jews and gentiles were needed—the gentiles to rebuke the unbelief of the Jews and the Jews to clarify the premonitions of the gentiles. Working together, they came up with the right answer, which neither would have discovered on their own.

Of great importance to John was the fact that the magi had come to worship the child, an act that no Jew would have considered and that some in the early church also called into question. John did not hesitate to use the story in order to condemn the second-century heretic Marcion, who rejected the witness of the Old Testament, and the third-century Paul of Samosata, who apparently believed that Jesus was no more than a man who was subsequently divinized. The wise men, according to John, knew better. They worshiped the child as God, validating the prophecy of Micah and rejecting the idea that Jesus was no more than a divinized man. The nativity story thus had a direct application to the controversies surrounding Christ that rocked the early church, and John was not slow to exploit that fact.[13]

JOHN'S DOCTRINE OF CHRIST

In his exposition of the Gospels, John was never in any doubt that Jesus Christ was the incarnate Son of God who had come into the world to save sinners. Everything Jesus did during his earthly ministry was an act of condescension, born out of the love of God for the fallen human race. In the sermons on Matthew he seldom spoke of that directly, even when the text gave him the opportunity to do so, but preferred to emphasize the Savior's humanity, as can be seen in his explanation of the temptations of Jesus in Matthew 4. When Satan tried to get him to turn stones into bread, Jesus replied that "man shall not live by bread alone," an answer that John claimed was deliberately designed to set an example for his followers: "Christ, to show that the virtuous man is not compelled ... to do anything that is unseemly, first hungered, then refused to submit, thereby teaching us not to obey the devil in anything."[14]

Even when Jesus admitted that he was God, he almost always did so in a way that demonstrated his great humility and forbearance, qualities that he sought to inculcate in his disciples. Thus when rebuking the devil, he quoted the Scriptures, giving us an example of how we should behave when Satan comes to tempt us. Later on, when Peter confessed to Jesus that he was the Christ, the Son of the living God, Jesus recognized the truth of what he was saying, but rather than dwell on it, he focused on Peter and told him that his faith was the rock on which he would build his church.[15] John explained this as follows: "Why did Jesus not just say 'I am the Christ,' but rather established this fact by questioning his disciples in a way that would lead them to confess it? Because to do that was more his style, one that was necessary at the time, in order to bring them into a deeper conviction of [the truth of] what was being said."[16]

It is not difficult to see how John interpreted the self-revelation of Jesus in terms of an evangelistic technique that we can still use today. People who might be put off by an open declaration of the truth can be drawn in by questions that force them to make up their own minds, and thus come to a deeper faith.

The Fourth Gospel takes a completely different approach to the origin and identity of Jesus than the one we find in Matthew, and it is here that John's theological acumen is most obviously on display. John the Evangelist does not dwell on the human ancestry of Jesus but goes immediately to the source: "In the beginning was the Word, and the Word was with God, and the Word was God" (John 1:1). Faced with such a bold statement as this, John Chrysostom had no choice but to address the philosophical and theological questions that it raised, and in so doing to demonstrate the logic of the Nicene orthodoxy that was even then imposing itself on the church.

John began by pointing out that the Fourth Gospel makes a clear distinction between the *being* of God and his *acts*. The Word *was* with God in the beginning. It was not created, either by a decree of the Father or out of some preexisting substance. As John pointed out, the verb "to be" has a relative meaning in the world of time and space, but in the context of God it corresponds to his eternity. To say, therefore, that the Word was with God was to say that he was *always* with God—there can be no "before" or "after" in him.[17] The contrast with the created order could not have been greater, and as we have already seen in the exposition of the creation in Genesis, John did not hesitate to make this point when talking about John 1.

At the same time, of course, the Word is not simply another name for God. He was *with* God and fully divine, but he was a distinct entity in his own right. Furthermore, it was the Word, not the undifferentiated "God," who became incarnate, a fact that clearly demonstrated both their difference and their fundamental equality. John was aware that on the day of Pentecost, Peter stood before the crowds in Jerusalem and told them that the man they had crucified had subsequently returned from the dead, and that God had made him both Lord and Christ (Acts 2:36). He knew that there were people who interpreted this to mean that God conferred divinity on Jesus after his crucifixion, an idea that strikes us as odd, but that would have sounded perfectly normal to many pagans, who were used to the divinization of fallen heroes. John countered this by pointing out that the titles "Lord" and "Christ" were not attributes of his divinity, but terms that express the dignity that has been conferred on him. The one who is God in eternity became Lord and Christ in time and space, because those titles have meaning only in the context of his relationship to us. In Jesus Christ heaven and earth are united, but they are not confused—the two natures coexist in the single person. John did not put it quite like that, because he lived more than a generation before that formula was devised at the Council of Chalcedon in 451, but it is clear from what he did say that had he lived to attend that council, his voice would have spoken up in favor of what would become its accepted orthodoxy.[18]

It is also worth noting here that John spent a good deal of time on demonstrating the divinity of the Holy Spirit in addition to that of the Son. This was occasioned by popular controversy that had broken out in his youth and that had been formally resolved at the First Council of Constantinople in 381, little more than a decade before these sermons were preached. In our world of instant communication, that seems like a long time, but news traveled slowly in the ancient world. Even after ten years, the deity of the Holy Spirit would not have been taken for granted by everyone in his congregation, and there may have been some who openly rejected it. It was therefore necessary for John to expound it at some length, even though it is not immediately obvious that the passage on which he was preaching is talking about the Spirit's divinity.

The question came up because of a popular misreading of John 1:3–4. It says, "All things were made through him, and without him was not any thing made that was made. In him was life." Some readers took that last part of this sentence and attached it to what follows, rendering it as: "What was made in him was life" and applied "life" to the Holy Spirit. John agreed with that part—the Holy Spirit was indeed a source of life, and that made him God, but not with the reordering of the sentence. The Son did not create life in himself and then breathe it out as the Spirit. Rather, the Spirit is eternally life and the bestower of eternal life on us. John went on to point out that if this misreading were to be followed through the rest of the passage, it would end up saying that it was the Spirit that became flesh and not the Son, which is clearly not the case. So instead of falling into errors of that kind, he argued that the only proper exposition of the verse was to allow for the divinity of the Holy Spirit alongside that of the Father and the Son—a Trinity of persons, even though the text does not explicitly say so.[19]

Following the logic of the passage, John went on to say that the light of Christ is given to everyone who comes into the world. It is in effect the substance of the image and likeness of God that we have received by virtue of our creation. But magnificent as this is, the sad fact is that human beings have rejected the light given to them and preferred darkness. In this way we are all responsible for our own sins. There are no grounds for supposing that one group of people has been exempted from this curse, or for suggesting that the light shines brighter in some than in others. All have sinned and come short of the glory of God, just as the salvation brought by Christ is available to everyone. Distinctions between Jews and Greeks, slaves and free, males and females—all of these differences are secondary and immaterial. The universality of sin has found its counterpart in the universality of salvation, which is available to all who desire it. Of course not all do, because not all are enlightened by the Spirit, but this is not because the salvation on offer is restricted to certain kinds of people. On the contrary, it is because human beings are free to go their own way, and many have used that freedom to reject Christ, oblivious of the great blessings that await them.[20]

One of the more interesting christological passages in John's sermons is found in his exposition of Jesus' encounter with the Samaritan woman in John 4. John knew quite a lot about the Samaritans and was well aware of Jewish attitudes toward them. He fully understood how odd it was that Jesus should have a conversation with the woman at the well, and he was particularly struck by the fact that Jesus revealed more about himself to her than he did to Nicodemus, whose theological credentials were so much more impressive. But John was astute enough to ask how the Samaritan woman knew about the coming of the Messiah and could claim that her people were waiting for him to come just as much as the Jews were. The Samaritans rejected the prophets and regarded only the Pentateuch as Scripture, but did Moses say anything about the coming of Christ?[21] Indeed he did, claimed John:

Even in the beginning, God revealed his Son. "Let us make man in our image, after our likeness" (Genesis 1:26) was said to the Son. It was the Son who talked with Abraham in the tent (Genesis 18), and Jacob prophesied concerning him when he said: "A ruler shall not fail from Judah, nor a leader from his thighs, until the one for whom it is reserved comes, and he is the expectation of the nations" (Genesis 49:10 LXX). Moses himself said: "The Lord your God will raise up a prophet for you from among your brethren; he will be like me and you will listen to him" (Deuteronomy 18:15). And the circumstances surrounding the serpent, the rod of Moses, Isaac, the sheep and many other things could have been chosen as evidence for his coming.[22]

It was the Jews who did not listen to Moses; the Samaritans, whom they despised and rejected, had received the same message, and in the case of this woman, at least, they seem to have accepted it more willingly (see Luke 16:19–21).

John never denied the divinity of Christ, nor did he minimize his saving mission. If there is some truth in the criticism that he paid less attention to these matters than some of his contemporaries did, it was not because of unbelief or lack of interest in them but because his focus was somewhat different. As a preacher, John was primarily concerned with the spiritual state of those to whom he was speaking. It was his job to make them willing imitators of Jesus in their own lives, and overemphasizing his divinity might have discouraged them from trying to do what might have looked like the impossible. John's approach was to present Jesus as the sinless man, whose teaching and way of life could serve as a model for his followers. To be sinless he had to be God; to be an example for others he had to be a "normal" man. In the person of Jesus of Nazareth, the Son of God had accommodated himself to the limitations of the human race and in doing so he had pointed the way by which those who had faith in him could rise to the eternal life of heaven.

John was particularly interested in the way in which Jesus responded to needy people with whom he came into contact. When the centurion approached him on behalf of his servant who was seriously ill with the palsy, and compared his own authority to that of Jesus, who (in his opinion) was able to issue a similar command and be obeyed, Jesus praised him and did exactly as the centurion wished (Matt 8:5–13). The same thing happened with the leper who approached Jesus and said that if Jesus wished, he could heal him. Again Jesus responded favorably and granted the man's wish (Matt 8:1–3). But when Martha, who was a friend of Jesus and knew him in a way that neither the centurion nor the leper did, said to him that whatever he asked God for would be given to him, she was rebuked (John 11:22). Why? Because she apparently thought that Jesus would have to ask someone else for the power and favor to heal and was not able to do it himself. In other words, thought John, Martha was effectively denying his divinity, an error that might have cost her the blessing she sought had Jesus not stepped in to correct her. The overall lesson John drew from comparing these three incidents was that faith in Jesus has the power to heal and that human familiarity with him was no substitute for that. The message being communicated here is that the Jews who had the law and the promises were not better off than the gentiles, who had nothing to rely on but their faith.[23]

Another example of Jesus' pastoral style can be seen in the healing of Peter's mother-in-law (Matt 8:14–15). Unlike the leper, she did not approach Jesus for healing and probably could not have done so, but others interceded with him on her behalf, just as the centurion did for his servant. John used this to tell his congregation that "Christ grants the healing of some to the faith of others."[24] As Christians we pray not only for ourselves but also for those who cannot or will not approach Jesus directly, and we are assured that he will hear us. The Savior is not constrained by our infirmities, but where there is faith, he will respond. Of course, that does not excuse us when we know what is required of us. The two blind men of Jericho cried out to Jesus to give them their sight, and when Jesus heard them and saw their faith he granted them their wish. In John's view, they had shown themselves worthy to receive the gift that Jesus had to give, and it was this that he urged his congregation to emulate. Our relationship to Christ is a two-way street—he will heal us, but we must also show ourselves worthy by our faith and our commitment to him if we expect to share in his blessing.[25] This was not salvation by works, however. When Jesus healed people, he told them to go and sin no more, because of the danger that something even worse might happen to them if they did (John 5:14). John took this to mean that such people were saved by grace and not by their own works or merit, because if they had earned their healing they would presumably have been immune to future failure.[26]

The way this worked out in practice could and did vary from case to case. Peter's mother-in-law and the centurion's servant were healed immediately, but not all situations were alike. The cripple at the pool of Bethesda was questioned about his circumstances before he was healed, a fact that John attributed to the amazing wisdom of God, who delayed the cure so that he could first establish a relationship with the man and make room for him to have faith.[27] But of all the relationships that Jesus had, the one with Judas was the most dramatic, and John's interpretation of it shows how far he was prepared to go in recognizing Jesus' flexibility in dealing with others. He pointed out that, far from condemning Judas outright, Jesus described him as one who had eaten bread with him, who had been fed by him, and who shared his table—stressing the positive side even when he knew that betrayal was at hand (John 13:18). But at the same time, Jesus also knew that his words could have been applied to the other disciples, and so he was careful to add that his words did not apply to all of them, but only to the one he pinpointed, a qualification that John believed was designed to put the minds of the others at ease.[28] But while Jesus told his disciples that he was the true vine, and that branches that did not bear fruit (like Judas) would be taken away, he also added that even those that do produce grapes will be purged, so as to improve their yield (John 15:2).[29] Jesus dealt with each case individually because the needs of each one of us are different, even if the reward of salvation is essentially the same. In this way, Jesus modeled the art of the pastor and set us an example of how we too must approach the great variety of people who come to us in search of their eternal salvation.

JESUS AS PASTOR AND SPIRITUAL GUIDE

John came into his own as a preacher when he stopped to consider Jesus as a pastor and spiritual guide to his followers and to those with whom he came into contact. This can be seen most clearly in his exposition of the Fourth Gospel, which is heavily weighted toward his encounters with people like Nicodemus and the Samaritan woman, and relatively light on the theological discourses that take up so much of the text.[30] John was evidently most at home when dealing with people, and he saw Jesus in much the same light. His starting point was the reality of sin, which he knew was universal and (in human terms) incurable.

Even in his exposition of the Matthean genealogy of Jesus, John pointed out that the unusual inclusion of certain women in the list was designed to make this point:

> The Jews paraded the name of Abraham, thinking that they could plead their ancestor's virtue, but Matthew shows that this gives no ground for boasting ... all are under sin, including their forefathers. Their own patriarch and namesake [Judah] committed a serious sin, for Tamar stands there to accuse him of his whoredom. David too had Solomon by the wife whom he corrupted. Now if the law was not fulfilled by the great men, how much more sinful would the lesser ones have been? And if the law was not fulfilled, all have sinned, and Christ's coming became necessary.[31]

The fundamental importance of this fact was underlined by the mission of John the Baptist, who came to prepare the way for the coming of Jesus. John was a kind of reincarnation of the prophet Elijah, but unlike his prototype, he had a very specific mission, which was to preach baptism for repentance, which must precede the forgiveness of sins. Even those who keep the law need to repent and be forgiven, because sin goes deeper than the commands of the law are able to reach. That is why Jesus submitted to John's baptism. He, alone among the people of Israel, had kept the law down to the last letter, but he sought baptism in order to "fulfill all righteousness" because keeping the law was not enough.[32] Today we might argue that Jesus did not need to be baptized because he was the sinless God, but although that is certainly true, it was not what John wanted to emphasize. The point that he was trying to make was that although Jesus was born under the law and kept it, the law was unable to save even the most perfect person. Jesus' baptism was not for his benefit but for ours, so that we would learn not to put our trust in precepts, which, however good they are in themselves, are still not enough to save us.

John also insisted that his namesake's baptism was for repentance only; it had no power to forgive sins, which was something that only God could do. Forgiveness is a spiritual act that cannot be produced by mechanical human actions, however important and necessary they may be. John believed that it was the human's part to repent and God's to forgive, as Jesus explained to Nicodemus when he said that unless we are born again of water and the Spirit, we cannot see the kingdom of God. As far as water baptism is concerned, John saw no difference between the Baptist and the Messiah—the physical act was the same in both cases and contained the same restricted message. What Christ added to John's baptism was the presence of the Holy Spirit, who brings with him the saving grace that we need in order to be born again.[33] John did not say whether Christian baptism was always or necessarily regenerative, though in principle it was baptism by water and the Spirit. What is remarkable about his approach is that he was aware that the two things did not always go together, even if he was reluctant to press the point for fear that his hearers would discount the significance of their baptism in Christ. But John was fully aware that there were professing Christians who led evil lives, thereby denying their faith and calling the efficacy of their baptism into question.[34] John did not dwell on such an embarrassing subject, but he knew that it was a problem and that its existence made it difficult for him to claim too much for the regenerative effects of a baptism that had been received unworthily. Here we see how pastoral experience trumped theological theory, and that John was unwilling to allow the latter to blind him to the realities forced upon him by the former.

The universality of sin and the equality of all human beings before God did not prevent some people from thinking that they had (or ought to have had) more pull with Jesus than others. Chief among these was his mother Mary and to a lesser extent his immediate human family. John was well aware of this way of thinking, which was common in ancient society and can still often be found today. He did not want to suggest that Jesus had any disrespect for his mother, but neither was he influenced by anything like the Mariolatry that later generations were to adopt. Commenting on Matthew 12:46–49, where Jesus pointed away from Mary and his brothers and declared that all his followers were equal to them, John had this to say:

> We know that Jesus took great care of his mother, because even on the cross he committed her to the Beloved Disciple and charged him to take care of her. But in this place he does not do that, and this out of the same sense of care for her and for his brothers. They looked on him as a mere man and had a sense of entitlement toward him. In response to that, Jesus cast out that disease, not by insulting but by correcting them. ... He did not want to confuse them but to deliver them from their obsession and to guide them little by little toward a right understanding of himself. He wanted to convince Mary that he was not just her son but also her Lord, and seen in that light, his rebuke to her, which is full of gentleness, reflects extremely well on him and is useful to her as well.[35]

Later on, when preaching about the wedding feast at Cana, John said much the same thing about Jesus' approach to his mother. Noting that Mary had interrupted the celebrations and tried to dictate to Jesus what he should do about the lack of wine at the feast, John remarked that she had stepped out of line and needed to be corrected. Her personal wishes could not come before the needs of the crowds who gathered around him, and Jesus knew that if he gave in to her request he would be disliked by the wider community for his apparent favoritism. By rebuking her as he did, he demonstrated that he cared for her soul more than for anything else, and at the same time that his mission was to do good for the many, and not just for the few who could claim to have his ear.[36]

John's remarks on the miracle at Cana are interesting for another reason, because John shares with us some of the common questions that it raised in the minds of his hearers. They wanted to know why Jesus went to the trouble of getting the servants to fill the jars with water instead of simply producing the wine straightaway, which (to their minds) would have been a greater miracle. John agreed with that, but answered that Jesus frequently lessened the greatness of his miracles, so that they would be easier for people to accept. In theory, producing something out of nothing would have been more impressive, but that would have been rather like a magician pulling a rabbit out of a hat. The suspicion would always have been that the wine had been hidden somewhere and produced "as if by magic." By changing already existing water into wine everyone could see that a miracle had occurred because they had witnessed an actual change of substance. John also made the point that Jesus took care to involve people in his activities as much as possible. He did the miracles, to be sure, but they also participated in the action, and in that way felt that they "owned" the result more than they might otherwise have done.[37]

John also came back to the core doctrine of creation, which he knew to be under attack from the so-called gnostics, who believed that the Creator God was a deity inferior to the Father of Jesus Christ, our Redeemer. Their argument was that there was something wrong with the created order that had to be overcome. John's reply to them was as follows:

> Since there are some who say that the creator of the world is another being, to curb these men's madness Jesus did most of his miracles by using matter that he found at hand. Had the creator of these things been opposed to him, he would not have used what belonged to someone else in order to demonstrate his own power. It was to show that he is the one who changes water into vines and who turns the rain, by its passage through the roots, into wine, that he expedited the process by doing in an instant at the wedding what would normally take the plant a long time to achieve.[38]

In other words, what Jesus did was supernatural, not antinatural; he took what nature has to offer and went beyond it, but without suppressing or denying its part in the overall work of salvation.

What is wrong with the world is not its material nature but the sin in our lives that cuts us off from God. John understood that Jesus' mission was to deliver us from the curse of that sin and explains the course of his life and ministry. He was very clear about this: "The Son of God came to rid us of our slavery to sin. That is why he took on the form of a slave, why he was spat upon, why he was physically assaulted, why he endured a disgraceful death. We must not nullify all this by going back to our former unrighteousness, or rather, by falling into something even worse. To serve the creature it is not necessary to bring the Creator down to the creature's level."[39]

Typically, John drew a direct line from the original purpose of Jesus' coming, through what he did when he was among us, to how we must now respond to what he has done for our benefit. Without Jesus, salvation would have been impossible, but without our participation in his achievement, it is pointless. Jesus came not only to set us free from the mistakes of the past but to transform us for the life of the future. The rest of the sermon is given over to particular instances of bad behavior that stand in need of correction. To the inattentive reader, much of what John said has little or no bearing on the text that he was expounding, but to John and his hearers, it was the most important thing. Without the newness of life that only Christ can bring, the gospel is effectively denied because there is nothing to show for it. For John, the proof of the resurrection of Christ lay as much in the transformed lives of those who believed in him as it did in any exploration of the historical evidence for an empty tomb. Once again, we see the practical concerns of a preacher and pastor coming to the fore, and the life and teaching of Jesus is interpreted primarily in the light of them.

Why did God choose the way of salvation that he did? Could he not have forgiven us without subjecting his Son to the pain and suffering that he endured? If sin and salvation are both spiritual realities more than anything else, why was the material world involved to the extent that it was? What was the point of the incarnation, and why does the church celebrate divine mysteries with material substances like bread and wine? Questions like these are not unknown even today, but in John's world they were especially pertinent. For the ancients, life was a daily struggle against the elements. Disease was widespread, mortality rates were high, and physical disabilities usually condemned the sufferers to a life of misery and exclusion from society. To pagan philosophers, the mind offered an escape from both pain and drudgery through philosophical contemplation, and the more that was practiced the happier a man (or much less often, a woman) would be. But the gospel is not a case of mind over matter. John understood that the Son of God had not simply forgiven our sins from a great height, but that he had entered our world and borne those sins in his own body. This was a degree of suffering and identification with us that no philosopher had achieved, or even considered, and it made all the difference.[40]

It is the common failing of the human race to place more emphasis on bodily pain than on spiritual alienation from God, and John did not hesitate to censure such inverted priorities. But he did not fall into the trap of saying that we should concentrate on saving souls and ignore the needs of the body. The miracles of Jesus were designed to show that the Savior has come to heal both flesh and spirit, and that salvation is not complete if one occurs without the other. It is, of course, true that nowadays spiritual healing is more readily available than its physical equivalent, but we must not be misled by this. A restored soul is prepared for eternity, whereas a restored body will eventually die. Its true healing will occur in the resurrection, when those who have been renewed in spirit will be reunited with their bodies in the kingdom of heaven.[41] Physical healing without spiritual renewal is a deception, because when the body eventually decays and passes away there will be no redeemed spirit to raise it up to a new life.

John also believed that when Jesus performed miracles of physical healing he was overcoming the limitations of the law of Moses, which had told people not to touch unclean things and prescribed detailed procedures to be followed in dealing with lepers and social outcasts generally. But Jesus, when he healed a leper, stretched out his hand and touched him, showing by his action that the man was not to be regarded as unclean.[42] Of course, this is a picture of spiritual redemption, because the person who is cleansed from sin is no longer unclean in the sight of God, who has touched us with the saving power of his grace. This is the radical power of the gospel to save those who believe and to make them acceptable in the sight and presence of God.

JESUS AS REDEEMER

John fully understood that the preaching and teaching ministry of Jesus was but the prelude to the great work that he would accomplish by dying for us on the cross. To his mind, every word of blessing and sign of healing pointed in the same direction. This is perhaps most obvious in his sermons on John 3, where the Gospel itself compares the crucifixion to the healing brought by the bronze serpent that Moses lifted up in the wilderness. When Jesus spoke to Nicodemus he did not hesitate to say that people must be born again by water and the Spirit if they hope to see the kingdom of God. John did not hesitate to connect this with baptism, but he went on from there to point out that Jesus lost no time in directing Nicodemus from that blessing to another, which gave baptism its meaning. That second blessing was the cross, and the two were closely connected, as Paul reminded the Corinthians (1 Cor 1:13). In John's words, "these two things declare more than anything else the inexpressible love of Christ, who both suffered on behalf of his enemies, and after having died for them, freely bestowed on them in baptism the complete forgiveness of their sins."[43] Not that John thought that baptism possessed some magical power of its own. He saw no material difference between John the Baptist's baptism and that of Jesus, which to his mind had the same purpose and the same limitations: "Both were alike without the gift of the Spirit. Both John's disciples and those of Jesus had one reason for baptizing, which was to lead the baptized to Christ. In order not to have to go running around trying to gather believers together, as Andrew brought Simon and Philip Nathanael, they instituted baptism, so as to draw everyone to themselves quite easily and to prepare the way for their future faith. But the baptisms themselves were the same; one was not superior to the other."[44]

John was well aware that there were bad Christians and that outward conformity to the church's requirements was no substitute for living a godly life in the Spirit.[45] It was the presence of the Holy Spirit in the life of the believer that made it possible for him to surpass the righteousness of the scribes and the Pharisees. John was clear that the Jews of Jesus' day had a degree of godliness. His argument was that if they did not, it would have made no sense to speak of a greater or a lesser form of it.[46] But whereas the Jews sought to please God by their works, Christians were set free from the law by the gift of a greater grace. No longer was the promise one of living to a considerable age in a land flowing with milk and honey, complete with the promise of many children and great wealth. The inheritance of the Christian was to be found not on earth but in heaven, in "adoption and brotherhood with the Only-Begotten" with whom we shall reign in glory.[47] There was admittedly still a place for human good works, but John understood this as part of the grace of God at work in us. It was his belief that God wants us to share with him in the attainment of our salvation, not by doing things that might prove us to be worthy of it, but in preparing ourselves to receive his gifts by adopting the right attitude. In his words, "God wants you to contribute a bit, so that the victory may be yours also. Just as a king wants his son to take part in battle ... even though the triumph is his alone, so God wants us to take part in the war against the devil. All he demands of you is that you demonstrate a sincere hatred of that enemy. If you give him that much, he will bring the war to an end by himself."[48]

Of course, you can only have the right attitude if the Holy Spirit is present and active in your life. Sharing in Christ's redemption is never an agreement between equals by which we deserve a share in his victory, but always (and only) a gift of his grace. Paradoxical as it may seem, the only way that we can obtain salvation is by submitting to him and accepting the fact that our reward is his achievement and not ours. According to John, this is why Christians do not pray for strength or wisdom as such, but rather that they may be filled with the Holy Spirit, who works in us the very things that we cannot acquire by our own efforts.[49]

To appreciate the full import of John's teaching we must recognize that he was not writing abstract treatises about salvation by works as opposed to salvation by grace through faith alone. He was addressing a congregation that needed to be told what it had to do in order to ensure that God would work in their lives. Today we would express this in terms of personal relationship, a category that was not part of John's mental universe. He conveyed the same idea by telling his people that they must first be in spiritual communion with God, and that only once they were would they see God at work in their lives. If that communion were not there, God's work would come as a punishment because it would destroy the unregenerate element in us without our knowledge or participation. As he would have put it, God's victory over the devil would also be his victory over us if we were still Satan's slaves, because the servant is not greater than his master. Here there is a good example of something that we can understand and assent to once we grasp the context in which John was speaking and the nature of the language that he was using. To put our trust in God is not a work that deserves a reward but a denial of our own capabilities and an acceptance that if we are to be saved, he must do for us what we cannot do for ourselves. But at each step along the way, God leads us by the hand and shows us that we must also participate in his work. We are not like unconscious patients on a hospital bed who do not know what the surgeons are doing to them, but are actively aware of what is happening and following God's work in our lives as he does it.

This is a constant theme of John's preaching ministry. God works with us as a teacher works with his pupils. We must submit to his authority and trust in his power, but at the same time he guides us along the way and associates us with everything he does, so that we understand what he is doing and are united to him in a shared experience. That experience is crucifixion with Christ, which is the ultimate goal of the Christian life in this world and the perfect preparation for new birth in the next.

John did not have a sacramental theology in the later sense of the term, but he attached great importance to both baptism and the Lord's Supper as instruments by which Christ comes into the lives of believers, and reminding his congregations of this is a frequent theme in his sermons. Redemption was not merely something that happened long ago on a cross far away, but a living experience that brings spiritual healing and rebirth to those who partake of them. In this respect, believers today are in an even better position than those who knew Jesus in the flesh. Commenting on the woman who touched Jesus' clothes and was cured, he said,

> Let us also touch the hem of his garment, or better still, if we are willing, have him completely. For it is his body that is set before us now and not just his garment, nor are we

merely to touch it, but to eat it and be filled. Let us therefore draw near with faith, everyone who is ill. For if those
who touched his garment drew so much power from him,
how much more will those who possess him completely?
To draw near with faith is not only to receive the offering
but to touch it with a pure heart, as if approaching Christ
himself ... when you see the priest giving it to you, do not
think that it comes from him, but think that it is Christ's
hand that is stretched out [to you]. So when he baptizes,
it is not the minister who does this, but God who takes
hold of your head with invisible power. ... When God
gives birth, the gift belongs exclusively to him.[50]

But although John had a high view of both baptism and the
Lord's Supper, he never confused the outward signs with the
spiritual things that they signified. As he put it,

When we contemplate the mysteries [= sacraments], let
us not look at the objects set before us but rather keep
his teaching in our minds. His word cannot deceive, but
our senses are easily fooled. ... Since the Word says, "This
is my body," let us be convinced and believe that, and
look on it with the eyes of the mind. For Christ has not
given us anything material; what comes to us in material
form must be perceived by the mind—both the new birth
and the renewal. If you did not have a body, he would
have given you these things in an incorporeal form. It
is because your soul is contained in a body, he gives you
things that the mind perceives in the form of material
objects.[51]

John was also very quick to apply the pastoral practice of
Jesus during his earthly ministry to the needs of the church in

his own day. As he saw it, Jesus made no attempt to force his teaching on his disciples, and there were even times when he withdrew from them so as not to overburden them with spiritual truths that they could not as yet absorb.[52] The preaching of the gospel is often like this. People can only absorb one thing at a time, and they must be led gently along until the time comes when they are ready to accept the teaching in its fullness. This is why Jesus only hinted at his coming death until the right time came for him to explain it to his disciples: "With regard to the time, Jesus orders all things wisely. He did not tell his disciples [about his death] at the beginning, in order not to upset them, neither at the time itself, so as not to confuse them. It was only when they had received sufficient proof of his power and when he had given them great promises about eternal life that he introduced what he had to say about those things, often interweaving his teaching with miracles and commands."[53]

The same principle can be seen at work in the dialogue between Jesus and the Samaritan woman. Jesus began by asking her to draw him some water from the well, and she was puzzled that a Jew would expect a Samaritan to do such a thing. But when she mentioned that, Jesus shifted the subject to a higher level—she could give him physical water from the well, but he could give her spiritual water from heaven. The common theme of water recalls baptism, but that is not mentioned in the text and John did not press the point. What he wanted his hearers to understand was that the woman could not grasp spiritual things without a visual aid, as we would say today, but that Jesus' purpose was always to lead her (and by implication, us as well) from the things of earth to the kingdom of heaven.[54]

As John saw it, it was in this interplay between earth and heaven that the gospel of salvation in and through Christ had to be preached and understood. The core is always spiritual. Sin is an act of spiritual disobedience to God, carried out by spiritual creatures. Neither animals nor material objects are capable of sinning, just as neither of them can be saved either. But at the same time, the creation is part of God's plan and purpose. Human beings are created in God's image, but they are material as well as spiritual, binding the two realms together in their own being. For this reason, they are key to the salvation of the world, a salvation that is neither purely spiritual nor purely material. The incarnation of the Son as Jesus Christ was the proclamation that salvation had come to the whole earth, and that the material world would be redeemed and transformed into a spiritual reality, but one that was not disembodied. Rather, the body would be raised from the dead, just as Jesus of Nazareth was raised from the dead, and the material universe would be redeemed. As material beings in a material world, we make use of material things in our relationship to God—things like water, bread, and wine that were authorized and consecrated by Jesus himself. But these material things are not ends in themselves. They are means to an end that is far greater and more satisfying than any earthly pleasure can be. Salvation is therefore not a denial of the material world but a progress beyond it, using it as a guide but not mistaking it for the destination. In saying this, John captured the essence of the gospel message and dealt a deathblow to the purely spiritual and mental teachings of the Platonists and others who despised the material creation. Jesus Christ is both the Creator and the Redeemer, having been the one for the purpose of becoming the other, and those who believe in him have the joy of knowing that they share an integrated worldview in which everything can be received in its proper place as a gift from Almighty God.

CHAPTER 4

In the Footsteps of Paul the Apostle

PAUL THE ROLE MODEL

I t is well known that great preachers, like actors, learn much of their craft from acknowledged masters. We cannot say who taught John how to preach, though like most young men of his time he had a solid grounding in the art of rhetoric, which, along with a natural talent, may have been enough to make him a competent preacher, if not the outstanding one that he evidently was. What we do know, however, is that he had a very obvious model on whom he based his ministry and whose counsel he constantly followed. That model was the apostle Paul. Whether John was temperamentally similar to Paul is hard to say, but even if he was, their affinity lies elsewhere. Paul is the only New Testament figure who comes across to us as a fully human pastor and preacher. Peter certainly exhibits the traits of a colorful character, but we see him mostly as a somewhat overly enthusiastic disciple of Jesus who was prone to fall on his face, and then as the leader of the post-Pentecost church in Jerusalem. The apostle John conceals himself behind his work, and we can say little about him beyond surmising that he was the "Beloved Disciple" who is otherwise anonymous in the Fourth Gospel. Other people appear from time to time, but they play bit parts in the unfolding saga of the early church. Men like Philip, Stephen, James (but which one?), Timothy, Titus, and Jude cross the stage now and again, but it is difficult to reconstruct them as well-rounded characters in their own right.

Paul is different. We know him both through his own writings and the Acts of the Apostles, which allows for a certain amount of comparison and cross-checking. He has all the charisma of someone who had been a dedicated foe of the gospel but who was suddenly converted by a miraculous divine intervention. In later years, we see how the same passion that propelled him to persecute Christians was transformed into a determination to make amends by preaching the gospel to the ends of the earth. We follow him in success and failure, as he founded congregations across the Mediterranean and labored incessantly to ground them in their new faith. His controversies have become the stuff of which the church has been made; his solutions to the problems he encountered remain our standard guide to this day. John Chrysostom saw himself as closer to Paul than to anyone else in the New Testament because so much of his own ministry was similar to that of the great apostle. Like Paul, John had to deal with refractory congregations. Like Paul, he was faced with opposition from Jews who often appeared to have the weight of tradition on their side. Like Paul again, he was forced to deal with difficult pastoral problems on a daily basis. He was even summoned to preach before Caesar, albeit for very different reasons, though the eventual outcome was remarkably similar.

Just as Paul did not long survive his encounter with the imperial court, so John's career came to an end there too.

There were certainly differences between the two men and their respective circumstances, but the similarities are clear enough. Paul was the kind of witness to the gospel that John wanted to be, and he spared no effort in trying to make his own career conform as closely as possible to that of the great apostle. Not only did he comment on all fourteen epistles that make up the Pauline corpus (including Hebrews, which John accepted as Paul's work), but throughout his writings he quotes Paul abundantly and the lessons he draws from his teaching and example are almost too numerous to count. There were others in the early church who were drawn to Paul, including John's great contemporary Augustine and the anonymous Latin commentator known to us as Ambrosiaster, but they were unknown to him and their devotion to Paul was less explicit and less pervasive. The sixteenth-century Reformers were also attracted to Paul, albeit more for his theology of salvation by grace through faith alone than by his preaching or pastoral practice, and this helps explain why Chrysostom was so popular among them. Even today there is a Pauline bias in the modern Protestant church that makes John Chrysostom seem more accessible as a role model than most of the other church fathers. The Pauline tradition is alive and well, and preachers today can resonate with John to a degree that is not always possible with many of his contemporaries. The Cappadocian fathers (Basil of Caesarea, Gregory of Nazianzus, and Gregory of Nyssa), for example, were great theologians, but they can be hard to read and often appear remote from the concerns of ordinary people. John, on the other hand, while not as cerebral as they were, spoke the language of the street in a way that was relevant to people's everyday concerns. The failures of ordinary Christians and the role of the preacher in trying to admonish them and point them to follow a better way are themes that touch hearts more readily than learned discourses on the Trinity, important though the latter certainly are. The Cappadocians were intellectuals writing to and for other intellectuals, but John was a teacher of the masses, by no means un- or anti-intellectual, but with a practical bent that appeals far beyond the academy. In that respect, too, John's approach mirrors that of the apostle, and when we recognize it, the link between the two men appears more central and more meaningful to his work as a whole.

Paul held a special attraction for John because the apostle had taught his congregations to imitate him as he imitated Christ (1 Cor 4:16; 11:1; Gal 4:12). This gave John scriptural warrant for using Paul as a stepping-stone to Christ. Many people found it difficult to imitate the Savior directly, not least because as God in human flesh he was essentially inimitable. Paul, on the other hand, was a man just like us, warts and all. Yet in spite of his limitations, he was still able to portray himself as the model believers should follow in order to be like Jesus, and John made full use of this. John also knew that Paul had been based in Antioch, his own hometown, and that it was there that the followers of Jesus had first come to be known as Christians. John mistakenly thought that this was because Paul had spent so much time there, but although he was wrong on that point, there was no doubt that Antioch had played an important part in the apostle's life and mission.[1] John also lived at a time when the worldliness of the church was driving many to seek a purer form of their faith in the solitude of the desert. The monastic movement, as we now know it, was naturally drawn to Paul's advocacy of celibacy and freedom from the cares of this life, but Paul knew nothing of separation from the world and did not advocate it.

Given the circumstances in which John found himself, he cannot be blamed if he read Paul with the eyes of a monk, but it is not clear that he did. The similarities between Paul's outlook and that of the monks were accidental rather than deliberate, and John understood Paul well enough not to imagine that he was a genuine advocate of monasticism as this emerged in the third and fourth centuries.

What really attracted John to Paul was the apostle's pastoral flexibility. Like Jesus before him, but in some respects even more so, Paul adapted himself to a wide range of different situations and shaped his preaching accordingly. He wrote that he became a Jew to the Jews and a Greek to the Greeks, not in order to blend in with them or keep them happy, but so that he could present the gospel to them in a way that they would understand and might accept (1 Cor 9:20). It was that evangelistic purpose that drove him, and that so attracted John, who faced similar challenges in his own day. In terms of Pauline interpretation, John was more of a psychologist than a theologian. Those who read his sermons on the Pauline Epistles looking for what he had to say about grace as opposed to merit, or about justification by faith alone, are bound to be somewhat disappointed. It is not that Chrysostom denied these things, but his writings give the impression that he took them for granted and saw no need to expound them in any depth. When the subject came up, he naturally stated that we are saved by grace through faith and that our good works count for nothing before God, but since nobody (apart from Jews perhaps) was saying anything else he did not have to refute them in any detail. It was pastoral work that really moved John, as we can see from his sermons on Romans 16. To most modern commentators, the last chapter of Romans is an appendix to the rest of the epistle, which is where the heart of Paul's gospel can be found. John did not deny that, but for him, the list of names in Romans 16 had a special importance.[2] He did not know who the people were to whom Paul was referring, but he knew that they were real members of a living congregation, and that by naming them individually, Paul was demonstrating his pastoral concern for them. Far from being an appendix, the last chapter was the culmination of the whole, the justification for everything that had gone before. Paul was not just expounding doctrine—he was writing to particular people, and what he had to say to them was for their benefit. That is what John was doing in his own ministry, and what attracted him most to the example set by the great apostle.

John had been trained to believe that letters reveal the soul of their writers, and it was that which drew him most obviously to Paul. Through the epistles, he could commune with the man himself by entering into his inmost thoughts. Differences of approach that might seem contradictory to an outside observer could be accommodated, if not always harmonized, by an appeal to the complexity of the human heart and mind. We are often led to omit some things and emphasize others because of the audience or situation that we are confronting, and Paul's career was a perfect example of that. One minute he was circumcising Timothy so as not to cause needless offense to Jews; the next minute he was denouncing those in the church who maintained that circumcision was necessary in order to belong to it. John understood that this was not a contradiction, but evidence that Paul could adapt his practices to meet the needs of the moment. There was nothing wrong with circumcision in itself, and since Timothy had a Jewish mother, Jews would probably have expected him to have been circumcised just as they were. At the same time, circumcision was the sign of a promise given to Abraham, sealed under the law of Moses, and fulfilled by the coming of Christ. In the new dispensation it was redundant, and so to force it on believers was effectively to deny the power of the gospel that had come to replace it with a deeper understanding of our relationship with God and its consequences for our salvation.

John wanted to paint a portrait of Paul that would do justice to him as a pastor and preacher. Iconic representations of emperors and other public figures were common in the ancient world, and John drew on them as examples of what he had in mind. But his own practice was superior to that of a mere painter. A painter draws what he sees on the outside; John's concern was to reveal what he perceived on the inside—the soul of the man as revealed in his letters. When he talked about Paul's portrait he was really referring to his exegesis of the biblical texts that paint the picture for us—literary hermeneutics, not iconography, was what he was engaged in.[3] Modern readers must not impose their own preconceptions and expectations on John, and if they do, they will be disappointed. John must be read on his own terms and judged by the success or failure of what he was trying to do, not by criteria derived from the Reformers of the sixteenth century or their descendants. We must accept that John does not directly address many of our concerns, but the picture of Paul we get from him is not alien to our understanding either. In Chrysostom's work we see the apostle from a different angle, but one that is easy to accommodate within our own theological perspective. If we approach our subject in that way we shall not be deceived or disappointed but enriched by insights that might otherwise pass us by.

Finally, we must always remember that John saw Paul as a dialogue partner in his own pursuit of the gospel message. Time and again, he interrogated the apostle as if he were sitting in the room, wanting to know why he said one thing and not another, and then he went on, in good rhetorical fashion, to answer his own questions. Paul was a living presence for John, so much so that it was not unknown for icon painters of a later time to picture the two men together as master and pupil, with Paul standing over his disciple and telling him what to say. Later generations would often see John as Paul's most successful interpreter, because what he said he said out of his deep love for the apostle. To modern minds, such an approach may seem subjective and biased, but to those who believe in the communion of saints, it remains an inspiration and a model to emulate today.

THE INCOMPARABLE PAUL

John looked up to Paul as a role model, both for himself and for Christians in general, but at the same time he knew that in many respects the apostle was in a different league from him. Later generations would elevate Chrysostom to a similar level, but although John did his best to imitate his master he would hardly have thought of himself as his equal. As he said of Paul in the concluding paragraph of his introduction to his series of sermons on Romans, "This uneducated man overcame countless philosophers, stopped the mouths of countless orators, and did it all by his own quick wits and by the grace of God. What excuse then shall we have, if we are not equal to twenty names, and are not even of use to those who live with us? This is just a pretense and an excuse, for it is not want of learning or instruction that hinders our teaching, but drowsiness and sleep."[4]

John was obsessed with Paul and seldom passed up an opportunity to lean on the apostle's authority and example. He frequently digressed in his sermons to refer to him, even when the subject matter was quite different. Discoursing on Isaiah 45:7, for example, he felt called away as if by some supernatural force: "What is wrong with me? I have to do all I can to run away, because otherwise Paul will take hold of me and divert me from the passage I want to preach on. You all know how often this has happened in the past, how Paul has confronted me in the middle of my sermon, taken possession of me ... with such force that I was led by him to ruin the sermon completely."[5] As the evidence of his surviving homilies bears witness, John was a willing captive to this spiritual attraction. Time and again he brought the subject back to Paul and used him as the authoritative guide to interpreting what the text he was preaching on really meant. Of course, John recognized that Paul was an apostle, specially chosen by Christ for the task of preaching to the gentiles. He spoke with a sense of his divinely given authority, which he expected his congregations to hear and obey. He was also the author of a substantial portion of the New Testament, making his words the same as God's revelation to his people. No preacher of a later time could aspire to such heights, and in this respect John would have had to recognize Paul's uniqueness even if he had not been particularly taken with him.

But when we read John's sermons, we quickly realize that he went far beyond what Scripture itself said. Margaret Mitchell has counted no fewer than sixty-five epithets that John used to describe the superlative excellence of Paul, and only a handful of them have direct biblical warrant, although, as she points out, many of them are consonant with what the inspired text says.[6] For example, Paul called himself a "herald" of the gospel (1 Tim 2:7; 2 Tim 1:11) and so John claimed that he was a "heavenly trumpet," which amounted to much the same thing, expressed in slightly more colorful language.[7] Paraphrasing of this kind was common, and indeed necessary if John was going to maintain the momentum created by employing strings of laudatory epithets in the first place. Had he stuck to the evidence of Paul's own writings, he would have run out of material almost before he got started.

But John did not stop at biblical or semibiblical imagery. He was quite prepared to refer to Paul as "the mouth of Christ" and as "the lyre of the Spirit," neither of which had any biblical precedent.[8] At one point he even claimed that Christ used Paul to reveal things that were greater than anything that he himself had said during his earthly ministry.[9] One of John's favorite images of Paul was that of a bird that flew across the world at a great height.[10] Again, there was no biblical warrant for such a comparison, though it was a stock image of pagan poetry and rhetoric.[11] That did not seem to bother John, perhaps because he thought that in literary terms, Christianity was not so much opposed to paganism as vastly superior to it.

Nor did John mind borrowing rhetorical techniques from the essentially pagan culture of the Roman Empire. In a very detailed study of this phenomenon, Mitchell has demonstrated how he used the image of the imperial portrait, which was designed to blend the physical with the spiritual in a way that prefigured the later use of icons, in order to praise Paul.[12] On several occasions he drew attention to Paul's hands, to his feet, to his eyes, and even to his stomach. As Paul was first and foremost a preacher, his mouth came in for John's special attention, and John was not slow to praise it in the most extravagant ways, even to the point of saying that Christ sat on his tongue.[13] Whether his hearers tired of all this exaggerated praise is impossible to say, but John never did. For him, Paul stood head and shoulders above every other preacher, teacher, and evangelist—past or present. He even wrote seven sermons specifically in praise of the apostle, something that was unprecedented in ancient times.[14]

One curiosity of John's admiration for Paul is that he thought of him as a great athlete and soldier. We are not surprised that John should have seen the apostle as an extraordinary teacher and evangelist, and of course Paul did mention athletics and soldiering in the course of his letters. Even so, it is hard to imagine a bookish rabbinical student in Jerusalem taking much interest in either of those things, but John was not deterred by that. For him, Paul was an athlete who could wrestle, run, and box as well.[15] He was an unbeatable champion.[16] It is obvious that here we have left the historical Paul behind and found ourselves in a fantasy world of John's own imagining. What would the apostle have said if he had heard himself called not simply a soldier or a general, but even a gladiator?[17] Of course none of this detracts from Paul's exceptional gifts and achievements, which retain all their luster regardless of the ways in which John chose to praise them. But it is fair to say that few modern preachers would let themselves be carried away to that extent in praise of Paul. Perhaps this is because we are less rhetorical and more aware of history than John was, but it may also have something to do with a certain modern reluctance to engage people on their own terms. Even today, gifted athletes and successful military men are highly regarded in popular culture whereas scholars generally are not. John was speaking to people who admired physical strength and skill, and so he portrayed Paul to them in those terms. He did not see this as a distortion of reality, but as an adaptation to suit the way in which most people in his congregation thought. To take a modern comparison, picturing Paul as a champion footballer would be inaccurate in strictly literal terms, but it might speak to the kinds of people who do not read books—or go to church either, for that matter. That is what John was trying to do.

John's praise for Paul, overdone as it was, would have made no sense if the apostle had not taught the pure gospel of Christ and won scores of gentiles to the Christian faith. If John was infatuated with his hero, it was for a reason. John would not have agreed with those modern theologians who claim that Paul was the true founder of Christianity, but he would have understood how that particular distortion could arise. Without Paul, the church would have developed differently and might even have remained a kind of Jewish sect. Much of Paul's ministry was a struggle to break free from the confines of Judaism, not by rejecting it outright, but by transforming it into something more purely spiritual and therefore more readily applicable to non-Jews as well.

This mattered to John because if Paul had not succeeded in his aims, neither he nor most of his congregation would ever have become Christians. The message of salvation would have stayed within the Jewish community and been concealed, if not smothered, under a blanket of legal maxims that were designed to point the way to Christ but that the Jews were using as a substitute for embracing him. To convey the importance of this, Paul himself stressed the spiritual character, not only of the message he was proclaiming, but also of the messengers whom he appointed to proclaim it. Christian leaders were expected to exemplify the things they preached about, and churches were meant to be schools of virtue. It is impossible to read the Pauline Epistles, and especially those that were directed at congregations in trouble (like 1 and 2 Corinthians), without perceiving the intensely practical nature of so much of what the apostle was saying. He was not unconcerned with the deity of Christ or with justification by faith alone, but he believed that such teachings ought to produce men and women whose lives had been transformed for the better. Virtue was not a prerequisite for salvation—and in that respect John and Paul were both deeply opposed to the main philosophies of their time—but it was the expected result of it, and if it were missing, something about the message had gone wrong. Since the gospel was the truth, it cannot have been the problem. The trouble was that either it was preached by unworthy people, of whom there were many, or its implications had not been driven home sufficiently.

For John, Paul was the supreme example of someone who practiced what he preached. His message was divine revelation because he himself was an example of divine transformation in his own life. From being an enthusiastic persecutor of the church, Paul had become its chief advocate and evangelist, the man who more than any other had gone to the ends of the earth in order to bring the good news to the lost. People who met Paul encountered Christ, because Christ dwelled in him and they saw for themselves what the gospel could do, not just for the chief of sinners that he had been, but for them as well.

THE GOSPEL OF GRACE

John was an enthusiastic expositor of the Pauline Epistles, not least of Paul's great letter to the Romans. Paul was writing to a church that he had neither founded nor visited but that occupied a central place in the world of his time. The church there was mainly Jewish, but with plenty of gentile converts whose exact status was disputed. Did they have to become Jews as well as Christians, or was it possible to receive Christ as Savior without submitting to the demands of the Mosaic law? It is evident from what Paul said that many Jewish Christians were uncertain about this, and probably some were unhappy about accepting gentiles as fellow believers. In his epistle, Paul tackled the whole question of sin and salvation, starting with the creation of the world and continuing through the history of Israel and its fulfillment in Jesus Christ. It is thus the most comprehensive and coherent statement of Paul's gospel message that has come down to us.

John saw his own circumstances as remarkably similar to those of Paul and the Roman church of his day. Rome was still the center of the civilized world, the proud mistress of the Mediterranean Sea and its adjoining territories. It was wealthy and successful, but in spite of everything it had been conquered by the message of a few humble and semiliterate Galileans. Peter and Paul had both ended their lives there (as it was generally believed) in obscurity and disgrace, but by John's time they had become the spiritual masters of the city, and hence of the empire, which was an extension of it. John may have lived in Antioch, but he and his congregation were Roman citizens, familiar with the rituals of imperial power and immersed in patriotic customs of purely pagan origin. It was not until 380 that Christianity was made the official religion, so John's ministry coincided with the conversion of the state and its citizenry to the new faith. As the metropolis of the East, Antioch played a key role in this process and John did not hesitate to see himself and his people in the light of the Romans to whom Paul wrote. At the same time, Antioch was home to a large Jewish community that continued to attract pagans and disputed the claims of the Christian church to be the new and true Israel. Paul had refuted the Jews at length in his epistle, and his approach to them was of considerable practical importance to John. It does not seem that John targeted the Jews for conversion, but he did use Paul's exposition as an argument to put to gentiles who might have been persuaded by them. Circumstances had changed in the course of the centuries, but for John, the need to tackle both paganism and Judaism was as pressing as it had been for the apostle more than three hundred years earlier.

After reminding his hearers of the miracle of Rome's conversion, John insisted that in the church everyone, Jew and gentile alike, is equal in the sight of God. The love of God had sanctified both, and every member of the church was a "saint."[18] Furthermore, Paul told the Romans that he needed them as much as they needed him—belonging to the church was partaking in a fellowship that embraced everyone without favoritism.[19] This unity in Christ had been Paul's fundamental message, and it was even more relevant in John's day, when the vast majority of Christians were of gentile origin. The Jews were not a spiritual elite, and their pretensions were belied by the fact that even on their own terms they had failed to keep the law of Moses. They had tried to make themselves holy and righteous but had not been able to live up to the standard that the law required. Holiness and righteousness could not be acquired by works, however good they might be, but only by faith. Here it could be argued that the gentiles were actually superior. They had never known the law of Moses and could not be judged by its standards. They had a law of their own written on their consciences and kept it as best they could. It may have been inferior to the Jewish law in purely objective terms, but was it better to obey the demands of conscience or to fall short of the requirements of a written legal code? As John saw it, the truth was revealed when the gospel of Christ was preached. Many gentiles believed in Christ, and many Jews did not—evidence, if any were needed—of who had been closer to God all along.

At one point, John even claimed that God had originally revealed himself to the gentiles, and that it was only when they rejected him that he turned to the Jews as his chosen people. Later on, the process was reversed, when Jews refused to accept Jesus as their Messiah and the apostles turned back to the gentiles.[20] This rather strange argument was based on John's reading of Romans 11:30-32, which few people today would accept, but it is indicative of his general approach. To John, Judaism was a false solution to a real problem that affects the whole of humanity, and not just the one nation to whom the truth had been entrusted before the coming of Christ.

John based his argument for the universality of both sin and salvation on the original creation ordinances. The first human beings had disobeyed God's commands and had gone their own way, with the result that everything they said and did was corrupted. At the heart of this rebellion was the denial of human sexuality as this had been given by God. Instead of monogamous heterosexual intercourse, people had plunged into every kind of perversion, of which homosexuality was the worst because it was ultimately sterile.[21] Seeking pleasure, both men and women had abandoned the God-given ordinance by which it ought to be attained, and the result was bitterness and deception. Lies replaced the truth, and the creation suffered as a result. John never underestimated the seriousness of sin and its effects on us: "To offend God is worse than being punished for it. We are so perverted that if we had no fear of hell we would never choose to do anything good. ... We are condemned to hell, but if we loved Christ as we ought to love him we would realize that offending the one we love is worse than hell."[22]

It was when the human race had sunk to this condition that God called Abraham and established a covenant with him that eventually led to the law of Moses and the emergence of the Jewish people as we now know them. The law of Moses was counterproductive. In itself, it was perfectly good, but its commands were too great for anyone to be able to keep them as they should. As a result, the law condemned them for their failure, but had no means of saving them because mercy and forgiveness were alien to it. Furthermore, the law had what we would now call "built-in obsolescence." The patriarchs and prophets were fully aware that it was provisional, and they pointed to a future time when God would intervene and save his people in a way that the law could never do. Even the temple ceremonies, which Jews put so much store by, were a foretaste of what was to come in Christ. The Israelite priests had made atonement for sin by sacrificing the blood of sheep and calves, but they had no power to take away the guilt of sin. Their purpose was to point to Christ, the divine-human priest and sacrifice, who would make a full, perfect, and sufficient atonement for the sins of the whole world, with the result that the Jewish rituals were now redundant.

The key fact about Christ's atoning sacrifice is that it came from God and was in no sense a work of sinful human beings. The only way it could be received was by faith, and faith was open to everyone. As John put it, "Have no doubt. Justification is not of works but of faith. Do not reject the righteousness of God, because it is a double blessing. It is both easy and open to everyone."[23] Later on in his exposition, John said exactly the same thing when commenting on Paul's criticism of Jews who had rejected the gospel: "People are justified not by works, but by the gift of God. ... What was the point of the law? To make people righteous. But it had no power to do that, and no one fulfilled it. Everything in the law had the same aim—to justify people. ... But it was Christ who accomplished that aim through faith. If you have come to that faith you have not broken the law. On the contrary, you will have broken it if you do not turn to Christ."[24]

In one of his profounder insights, John told his congregation that according to Paul, faith was more demanding than works. The Jews thought that the physical effort required for good works was far greater than mere faith, which to their minds required no exertion at all. But John pointed out that faith demands a soul that is able to ward off the temptation of unbelief, a spiritual challenge that could be far greater than any physical labor.[25] John was nevertheless aware that the Christian who is justified by faith must demonstrate his new status by doing good works. In his words, "After receiving the grace of justification, we must live a life that reflects it. We shall do this if we love in earnest, because love is the mother of good deeds. Love is not just a word or a way of speaking, but a practical concern for others which is shown in works like relieving the poor, helping the sick, rescuing people from danger, supporting those in trouble, weeping with those who weep and rejoicing with those who rejoice."[26]

Were Christians enabled to do this because God's grace was imparted to them by some means that made them better individuals, or was justification rather imputed to men and women who remained the same sinners they had always been? This was one of the great questions of the Reformation, and the Reformers believed that John was on their side—justification was by imputation, not by infusion through sacramental grace. What did John think about that? It is a hard question to answer directly, because John did not use that kind of language—it had not been developed in his time—and had no idea of the later controversy that would emerge. But an answer can be given if we look at the bigger picture.

John believed (wrongly) that Adam and Eve were immortal beings who lost their immortality when they sinned.[27] That was his interpretation of Romans 5:12, which says that death spread to the whole world as a result of Adam's sin. But as John saw it (rightly), salvation in Christ is the gift of eternal life, but it is not a return to the Adamic state of immortality. For the Christian, eternal life is a future hope that will be realized through our own death and resurrection. In other words, believers are expected to perform the good works of justification in their mortal bodies, which in John's language meant that they are still sinners. This was his way of saying what Martin Luther meant when he said that Christians are "justified sinners," and so we are entitled to claim that on this key doctrine, the two men said the same thing. John knew very well that Christians are still sinners. Following

Paul, he told his congregation that when Jesus had put sin to death on the cross he had not changed human nature by abolishing sin altogether but had given us the power to overcome it in our lives.[28]

From a modern perspective, John was hampered by the inheritance of ancient Greek thought that he could not escape. This led him to embrace a false dichotomy between "soul" and "flesh" that forced him to argue, against the Greek tradition, that the flesh is not evil in itself because it was created by God and everything God made is good. On the other hand, John also had to agree with Paul that there is something called "carnal-mindedness," which he interpreted as surrender to the lusts of the physical flesh and not (as Paul intended) slavery to creaturely forces that are spiritually opposed to God.[29] It was an error common to most people of his time and helps to account for their preference for an ascetic lifestyle. Abstinence of all kinds was regarded as mortifying the flesh and getting closer to God. John understood that this was a spiritual struggle—fasting was not the same thing as going on a diet—but it was a struggle that had a physical dimension to it. Here we part company with him, although we respect his intentions and honor his attempts to put his beliefs into practice.

John's interpretation of Paul was colored by his background and cultural assumptions, but that is true of us all. The great thing about him is that we can strip those accretions away and still find the pure gold of the gospel at the heart of his message. In spite of his distance from us in time and space, John remains a precious witness of that gospel today, and we do well to heed his voice as he speaks to us across the centuries.

CHAPTER 5

The Legacy

John's career was cut short by exile and ended in disgrace. His "golden mouth" was silenced, and his followers were forced to undertake a lengthy pilgrimage to the heart of Cappadocia if they wanted to see him. It would not last. As long as John was alive he was a potential threat, and it was as the emperor was trying to distance John as far as possible from anyone he could influence that he succumbed to death in an obscure Asian town. But although the man was gone, his spirit lived on, and within a generation not only had he been rehabilitated at Constantinople, where his bodily remains were reburied with honor, but his sermons were also being copied and circulated all over the Roman world. For centuries, he would remain an inspiration and a model for those who came after him, though no one was ever able to equal his achievement. In Western Europe he was less well known, because his works were mostly not translated into Latin, but they were rediscovered on the eve of the Protestant Reformation. To the men who launched that movement he was a hero, the one who had confronted the powers that be and ultimately triumphed over them, even at the cost of his own life. But what the Reformers appreciated most was that John was a man of the Bible, whose mission was to expound the word of God and apply it to his hearers as the chief means by which they would grow in Christ. When Thomas Cranmer, archbishop of Canterbury (1533–1556), wrote the preface to the second edition of the Great Bible (in 1540), he quoted John at length and recommended his example to everyone who sought to know the truth of salvation in Christ. The words of John that Cranmer quoted can serve us perhaps better than anything else as a summary of his intentions and as the essence of his legacy to future generations of believers.[1]

> My common practice is to tell you in advance what I am going to talk about, so that you can pick up the Bible yourselves and read, weigh, and understand the subject matter, noting what I have already taught and what still remains to be proclaimed. That way you will be better prepared to hear what is still to come. I implore you, as I always will, that you should pay attention to what the preacher says, not only in church, but also at home. You must devote yourselves to the regular reading of the Holy Scriptures, something that I never tire of telling the members of my own household that they must do. Nobody should make the excuse that they are too busy with worldly affairs, nor should they say that reading the Bible is something reserved for those who have withdrawn from the world and dedicated themselves wholly to learning and religion. ... If you are engaged in the business of the world you have even more need of the Scriptures, because you are all the more exposed to spiritual danger. You are in the front line of the battle and so need

spiritual help and comfort even more than those who are far from the battleground and thus seldom wounded.

Just as hammers, saws, chisels, and axes are the tools of the craftsman's trade, so the Bible, the books of the prophets and apostles inspired by the Holy Spirit, are the instruments of our salvation. So let us not hold back from buying and reading the sacred text, and let us remember that it is more valuable to us than gold or silver. Just as thieves hesitate to rob a well-guarded house, so the devil and his angels will not dare to attack any place where the Holy Scriptures are to be found. Those who possess them are kept safe and know that they are protected, so that they can devote themselves to all good works and avoid what is evil. If they fail at any point, the Bible is there to speak to their consciences, and bring them to repentance.

Do not say that the Scriptures are too difficult for you to understand. The Holy Spirit has so ordered them that fishermen and shepherds can be edified by them just as much as learned doctors. ... The apostles and prophets wrote in a way that every reader might be able to understand them and perceive their basic message, which is the transformation of our lives. ... Take the book in your hands and read it again and again if you do not understand it at first. If you are still at a loss after that, ask someone who is better instructed than you are to explain it to you. Go to your pastor and preacher, be eager to learn, and I promise that if God sees that you are sincere, he will enlighten you by his Holy Spirit, even if there is no other person who can help you. ... The reading of Scripture is a great and strong protection against sin. Ignoring it, on the other hand, will only lead to your ruin and destruction.

Reading, studying, and applying the teaching of the Bible to our lives—this is the enduring message of John Chrysostom and his greatest legacy to the church. As we take our leave of him, let us do so in the words of the parting prayer that has come down to us as his final word to the church:

Almighty God, who has given us grace at this time with one accord to make our common supplication unto thee; and dost promise that when two or three are gathered together in thy Name thou wilt grant their requests: Fulfil now, O Lord, the desires and petitions of thy servants, as may be most expedient for them; granting us in this world knowledge of thy truth, and in the world to come life everlasting. Amen.[2]

Further Reading

John Chrysostom's works are only partially available in English translations, most of which were done in the nineteenth century and in a flowery style that makes them hard to read today. These can be found in *Nicene and Post-Nicene Fathers*, First Series, volumes 9–14, edited by Philip Schaff, originally published in 1889–1890 by the Christian Literature Publishing Company and reissued several times, most recently by Hendrickson Publishers, Peabody, Massachusetts, in 1994.

There is a respectable amount of secondary literature on him, though not as much as there is for his great contemporary Augustine of Hippo. Among the best and most comprehensive recent works are the following:

Kelly, J. N. D. *Golden Mouth: The Story of John Chrysostom, Ascetic, Preacher, Bishop*. 1995. Reprint, Grand Rapids: Baker, 1998.

Mayer, Wendy, and Pauline Allen. *John Chrysostom*. Early Church Fathers. New York: Routledge, 2000.

Mitchell, Margaret M. *The Heavenly Trumpet: John Chrysostom and the Art of Pauline Interpretation*. Louisville, KY: Westminster John Knox Press, 2002.

Rylaarsdam, David. *John Chrysostom on Divine Pedagogy: The Coherence of His Theology and Preaching*. Oxford Early Christian Studies. Oxford: Oxford University Press, 2014.

Notes

Chapter 1

1. John must have been born sometime between 344 and 354. The date 349 is the midpoint between these two, and its probability has been defended by J. N. D. Kelly, *Golden Mouth: The Story of John Chrysostom, Ascetic, Preacher, Bishop* (Grand Rapids: Baker, 1995), 296–98.

2. Six homilies on Isaiah 6 have survived in Greek, along with extensive fragments from Isaiah 1–8 and 10.

3. This number does not include Galatians, because what survives is a combined commentary on the entire book. It must originally have been a sermon series, which would bring the total number to well over 250.

4. It should also be remembered that Paul's home town of Tarsus is not far from Antioch and that Antioch was the base for Paul's early missionary journeys. The two men were almost compatriots, even though they lived more than three centuries apart.

5. It was a temporary reprieve, however; Eutropius was soon tracked down by his enemies and murdered, despite John's pleas for mercy to be shown to him.

6. The Matthew commentary has been translated into English by James A. Kellerman, *Incomplete Commentary on Matthew (Opus Imperfectum)*, ed. Thomas C. Oden, 2 vols., Ancient Christian Texts (Downers Grove, IL: IVP Academic, 2010).

7. Any similarities with modern academia are of course entirely coincidental!

8. John Chrysostom, *Homilies on John* 2.2. All translations of John Chrysostom are my own.

9. It must be remembered that John lived at a time before baptism had become universal and automatic. The people he baptized knew what they believed and understood that to become a Christian was to separate oneself from wider (pagan) society. It was only later, when the church and the wider society virtually

fused into one, that baptism was reduced to a formality dissociated from genuine spiritual power.

10. The Greek word *synkatabasis* is literally "condescension," a word that is sometimes used to describe this, though it tends to have a somewhat pejorative meaning in modern English. Another possibility is "adaptation." For a detailed study of the subject, see David Rylaarsdam, *John Chrysostom on Divine Pedagogy: The Coherence of His Theology and Preaching*, Oxford Early Christian Studies (Oxford: Oxford University Press, 2014).

11. For John, as for the apostle Paul, the terms "Jew" and "Greek" were religious more than ethnic descriptors, despite the obvious overlap between them.

12. John Chrysostom, *In principium Actorum* 4 (Patrologia Graeca 51:103). See Rylaarsdam, *Divine Pedagogy*, 191.

13. John Chrysostom, *Homilies on John* 34.2.

14. John Chrysostom, *Homilies on John* 41.1.

15. John Chrysostom, *Homilies on John* 55.2.

Chapter 2

1. However, Augustine knew about John, thanks to the fact that Jerome had included him in his book of heroes of the faith (*De viris illustribus*). See his *Contra Iulianum* 22 for his appreciation of Chrysostom and his witness to the faith.

2. We know from the texts that the second series was preached in Lent, probably in 388, which would place them in late February and early March, since Easter fell that year on April 9.

3. There are seventeen sermons in all on Genesis 1–3, numbered 2–18 in the existing collection.

4. John Chrysostom, *Homilies on Genesis* 2.4.

5. John Chrysostom, *Homilies on Genesis* 2.8, quoting Acts 17:24–25. In fairness, John might have added that the same idea was present among the Jews as well. Cf. Isaiah 66:1.

6. John Chrysostom, *Homilies on Genesis* 7.11.

7. John Chrysostom, *Homilies on Genesis* 3.3–4.

8. See John Chrysostom, *Homilies on Genesis* 3.7.

9. See John Chrysostom, *Homilies on Genesis* 3.8.

10. John Chrysostom, *Homilies on Genesis* 4.7.

11. To understand the significance of this, we have only to compare the Christian attitude with the Muslim one. Christians do not hesitate to translate the Bible, but Muslims insist that the

Qur'an cannot be rendered into any language other than Arabic because its meaning would then be lost.

12. John Chrysostom, *Homilies on Genesis* 5.10.

13. John Chrysostom, *Homilies on Genesis* 5.14.

14. John Chrysostom, *Homilies on Genesis* 6.18.

15. John Chrysostom, *Homilies on Genesis* 6.11–17.

16. John Chrysostom, *Homilies on Genesis* 6.22.

17. John Chrysostom, *Homilies on Genesis* 3.22.

18. John Chrysostom, *Homilies on Genesis* 8.4.

19. By way of comparison, John's contemporary Augustine of Hippo (354–430) interpreted this verse as a reference to the Trinity and claimed that God created Adam in Trinitarian form, with (for example) three parts to his mind—memory, intellect, and will. John did not go as far as that.

20. John Chrysostom, *Homilies on Genesis* 8.9.

21. John Chrysostom, *Homilies on Genesis* 8.9–10.

22. John Chrysostom, *Homilies on Genesis* 9.7.

23. John Chrysostom, *Homilies on Genesis* 8.14.

24. John Chrysostom, *Homilies on Genesis* 9.14.

25. John Chrysostom, *Homilies on Genesis* 10.2.

26. John Chrysostom, *Homilies on Genesis* 10.3–4.

27. John Chrysostom, *Homilies on Genesis* 9.7.

28. John Chrysostom, *Homilies on Genesis* 9.7.

29. John Chrysostom, *Homilies on Genesis* 9.9.

30. John Chrysostom, *Homilies on Genesis* 9.11.

31. John Chrysostom, *Homilies on Genesis* 10.9.

32. John Chrysostom, *Homilies on Genesis* 10.17–18.

33. John Chrysostom, *Homilies on Genesis* 11.1.

34. John Chrysostom, *Homilies on Genesis* 14.8–9.

35. John Chrysostom, *Homilies on Genesis* 12.13; 13.6.

36. John Chrysostom, *Homilies on Genesis* 12.17.

37. John Chrysostom, *Homilies on Genesis* 12.18.

38. John Chrysostom, *Homilies on Genesis* 13.13.

39. John Chrysostom, *Homilies on Genesis* 13.15.

40. He was however aware of the difficulty and promised his hearers that he would return to it at a later stage. See John Chrysostom, *Homilies on Genesis* 14.15.

41. John Chrysostom, *Homilies on Genesis* 14.17.

42. John Chrysostom, *Homilies on Genesis* 15.5.

43. John Chrysostom, *Homilies on Genesis* 15.8.

44. John Chrysostom, *Homilies on Genesis* 18.12.

45. John Chrysostom, *Homilies on Genesis* 15.14.

46. John Chrysostom, *Homilies on Genesis* 17.42.

47. John Chrysostom, *Homilies on Genesis* 16.3.

48. John Chrysostom, *Homilies on Genesis* 16.3.

49. John Chrysostom, *Homilies on Genesis* 16.6.

50. John Chrysostom, *Homilies on Genesis* 16.10.

51. John Chrysostom, *Homilies on Genesis* 16.13.

52. John Chrysostom, *Homilies on Genesis* 17.19.

53. John Chrysostom, *Homilies on Genesis* 16.15.

54. John Chrysostom, *Homilies on Genesis* 18.3.

55. John Chrysostom, *Homilies on Genesis* 16.17.

56. John Chrysostom, *Homilies on Genesis* 18.8–9.

57. John Chrysostom, *Homilies on Genesis* 17.6.

58. John Chrysostom, *Homilies on Genesis* 17.13.

59. John Chrysostom, *Homilies on Genesis* 17.26.

60. John Chrysostom, *Homilies on Genesis* 17.34.

Chapter 3

1. John Chrysostom, *Homilies on Matthew* 1.4.; 30.1.

2. John Chrysostom, *Homilies on John* 2.1.

3. John Chrysostom, *Homilies on Matthew* 1.7.

4. John Chrysostom, *Homilies on Matthew* 4.3.

5. John Chrysostom, *Homilies on Matthew* 1.5.

6. John Chrysostom, *Homilies on Matthew* 1.6.

7. John could have known the Nicene Creed, which was probably composed at (or shortly after) the First Council of Constantinople in 381, but how many of his congregation would have been familiar with it is uncertain. It was still far too new to have become a regular part of worship.

8. John Chrysostom, *Homilies on Matthew* 5.4.

9. The argument concerns the dating of the census, which does not seem to coincide with any reasonable date for the birth of Jesus.

10. John Chrysostom, *Homilies on Matthew* 6.3.

11. John Chrysostom, *Homilies on Matthew* 6.4.

12. John Chrysostom, *Homilies on Matthew* 7.1.

13. John Chrysostom, *Homilies on Matthew* 7.5.

14. John Chrysostom, *Homilies on Matthew* 13.3.

15. John Chrysostom, *Homilies on Matthew* 54.2–3.

16. John Chrysostom, *Homilies on Matthew* 54.2.

17. John Chrysostom, *Homilies on John* 3.3.
18. John Chrysostom, *Homilies on John* 3.3.
19. John Chrysostom, *Homilies on John* 5.1.
20. John Chrysostom, *Homilies on John* 8.1.
21. The Samaritans also accepted Joshua as Scripture, but apparently John did not realize that.
22. John Chrysostom, *Homilies on John* 33.2.
23. John Chrysostom, *Homilies on Matthew* 26.2.
24. John Chrysostom, *Homilies on Matthew* 27.1.
25. John Chrysostom, *Homilies on Matthew* 66.1.
26. John Chrysostom, *Homilies on John* 38.2.
27. John Chrysostom, *Homilies on John* 37.1.
28. John Chrysostom, *Homilies on John* 71.2.
29. John Chrysostom, *Homilies on John* 76.1.
30. Of the eighty-eight sermons, the first quarter (1–22) expounds 1:1–2:10, the second quarter (23–44) covers 2:11–6:27, the third quarter (45–66) deals with 6:28–12:24, and the last quarter (67–88) skates over 12:25–21:25, the chapters where the main theological expositions are to be found.
31. John Chrysostom, *Homilies on Matthew* 3.3.
32. John Chrysostom, *Homilies on Matthew* 10.1–2.
33. John Chrysostom, *Homilies on John* 17.2.
34. John Chrysostom, *Homilies on John* 28.2.
35. John Chrysostom, *Homilies on Matthew* 44.1.
36. John Chrysostom, *Homilies on John* 21.2–3.
37. John Chrysostom, *Homilies on John* 22.1.
38. John Chrysostom, *Homilies on John* 22.1.
39. John Chrysostom, *Homilies on John* 4.4.
40. John Chrysostom, *Homilies on Matthew* 11.6.
41. John Chrysostom, *Homilies on Matthew* 14.5.
42. John Chrysostom, *Homilies on Matthew* 25.2.
43. John Chrysostom, *Homilies on John* 27.1.
44. John Chrysostom, *Homilies on John* 29.1.
45. John Chrysostom, *Homilies on John* 28.2.
46. John Chrysostom, *Homilies on Matthew* 16.6.
47. John Chrysostom, *Homilies on Matthew* 16.6.
48. John Chrysostom, *Homilies on Matthew* 16.14.
49. John Chrysostom, *Homilies on Matthew* 55.8.
50. John Chrysostom, *Homilies on Matthew* 50.3.
51. John Chrysostom, *Homilies on Matthew* 82.4.

52. John Chrysostom, *Homilies on Matthew* 49.1; 55.1.

53. John Chrysostom, *Homilies on Matthew* 65.1.

54. John Chrysostom, *Homilies on John* 32.1.

Chapter 4

1. John Chrysostom, *Homilies on Acts* 25.1.

2. See John Chrysostom, *Homilies on Romans* 31.1.

3. This point is made forcefully and in great detail by Margaret M. Mitchell, *The Heavenly Trumpet: John Chrysostom and the Art of Pauline Interpretation* (Louisville, KY: Westminster John Knox, 2002).

4. John Chrysostom, *Homilies on Romans*, Argument (near the end).

5. John Chrysostom, *Homilies on Isaiah* 45:7 3.

6. Mitchell, *Heavenly Trumpet*, 91.

7. John Chrysostom, *Homilies on 2 Corinthians* 11:1 1; *Homilies on Acts* 25:1; *Homilies on the Statues* 1.1; *Homilies on Acts* 9:1 3.4. In his *Homilies on Romans* 1.1, he varies this by calling him "the spiritual trumpet." Compare also Rev 1:10, where John the Divine heard a voice like the sound of a trumpet, which may have inspired Chrysostom's analogy.

8. John Chrysostom, *Homilies on Lazarus* 6.9.

9. John Chrysostom, *Homilies on Romans* 32.3.

10. John Chrysostom, *Homilies on Genesis* 34.5.

11. Mitchell, *Heavenly Trumpet*, 77.

12. See Mitchell, *Heavenly Trumpet*, 94–134, for a detailed examination of this.

13. John Chrysostom, *Homilies on Romans* 32.3.

14. They are translated in Mitchell, *Heavenly Trumpet*, 440–87.

15. John Chrysostom, *Homilies on 2 Corinthians* 25.3.

16. John Chrysostom, *Homilies on Acts* 55.3.

17. John Chrysostom, *Homilies on Acts* 25.1.

18. John Chrysostom, *Homilies on Romans* 1, commenting on Rom 1:7.

19. John Chrysostom, *Homilies on Romans* 2, commenting on Rom 1:12.

20. John Chrysostom, *Homilies on Romans* 19, commenting on Rom 11:30–32.

21. John Chrysostom, *Homilies on Romans* 4, commenting on Rom 1:26–27.

22. John Chrysostom, *Homilies on Romans* 5, commenting on Rom 2:15.

23. John Chrysostom, *Homilies on Romans* 7, commenting on Rom 3:26.

24. John Chrysostom, *Homilies on Romans* 17, commenting on Rom 10:3–4.

25. John Chrysostom, *Homilies on Romans* 8, commenting on Rom 4:20.

26. John Chrysostom, *Homilies on Romans* 7, commenting on Rom 3:31.

27. In fact, Adam and Eve were mortal beings who lost their protection against death when they sinned. Had they been immortal in the way that angels are, they would have become like demons. They could not then have been saved, because it is impossible to die for an immortal being.

28. John Chrysostom, *Homilies on Romans* 11, commenting on Rom 6:10–12.

29. John Chrysostom, *Homilies on Romans* 13, commenting on Rom 8:7.

Chapter 5

1. John Chrysostom, *On Lazarus* (*De Lazaro*) 3.1, freely translated.

2. From the order for Evening Prayer, *Book of Common Prayer* (1662).

Subject Index

Scripture Index